D1573680

Copyright © 2023 Naty Osa. Illustrations Javier Durá Osa.
All rights reserved. No portion of this book, except for brief review, may be reproduced, stored in a retrieval system, or transmitted in any form or by any means—internet, digital, electronic, mechanical, photocopying, recording, or otherwise— without written permission of the publisher. For further information contact Stinky Press Publishing.
Published by Stinky Press Publishing.
Book design by Javier Durá Osa, Naty Osa
ISBN: 978-0-9890898-1-4
Library of Congress Control Number: 2022923860

How the Fish Got Its Tail

written by Naty Osa illustrated by Javier Durá Osa

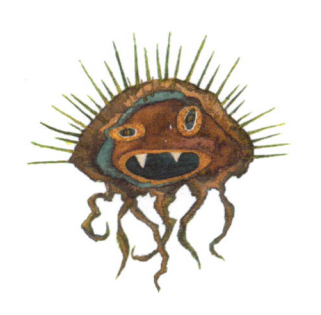

STINKY PRESS PUBLISHING
CHICO, CALIFORNIA
www.stinkypress.com

In a far away corner of the ocean deep
                              deep
                    deep
              deep
      deep
down in the deepest darkest trench
lived a colony of jelliballs.

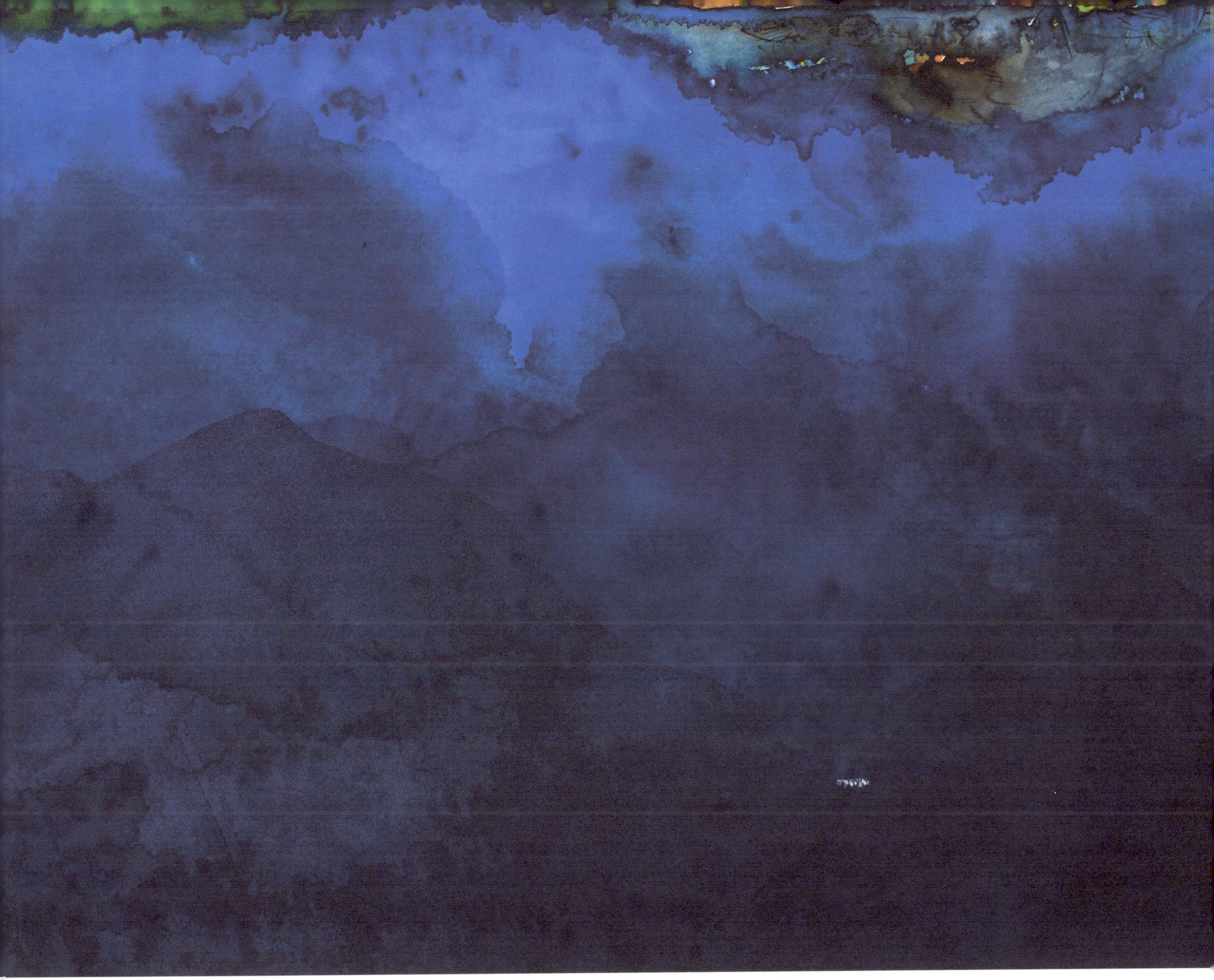

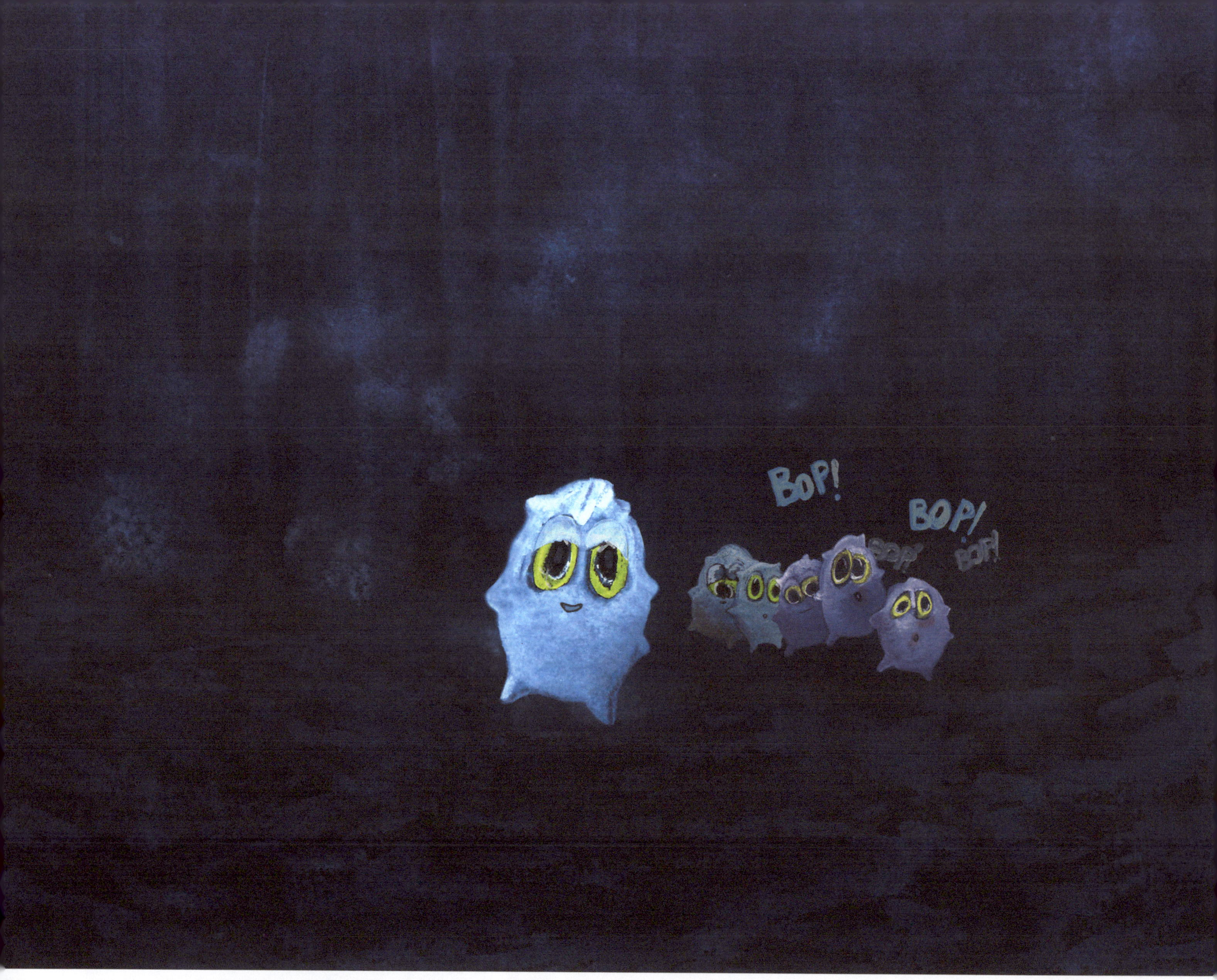
BOP!
BOP!

Even inside your closet with the door closed and your eyes squeezed shut, you couldn't make it that dark. Still, Bobi and the jelliballs did normal jelliball things, chattered in jelliball talk, played jelliball games, and told jelliball jokes.

"It wasn't always so." There was some wriggling and jostling as the jelliballs clustered around Grandpa for story time. Bobi was always in the front row.

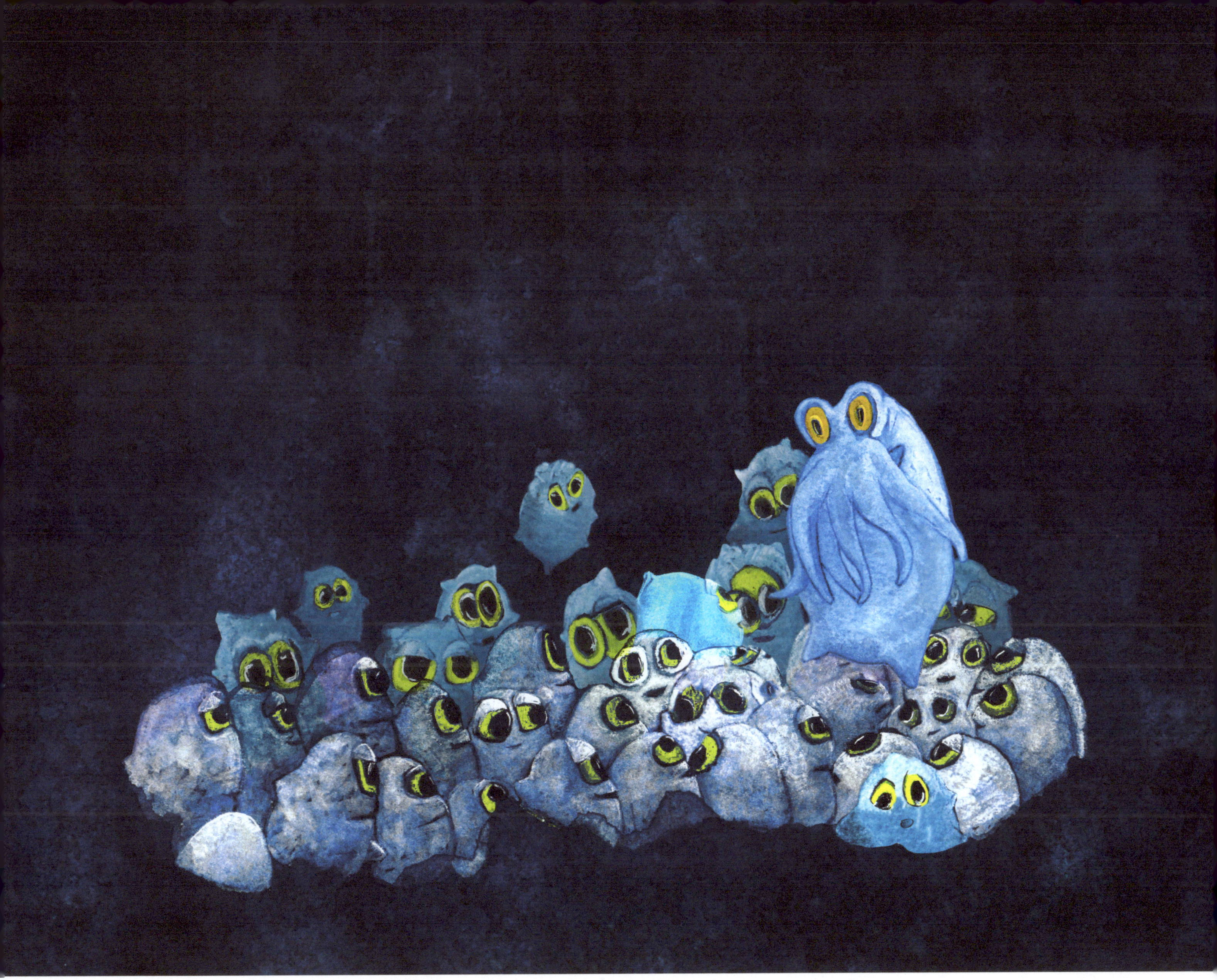

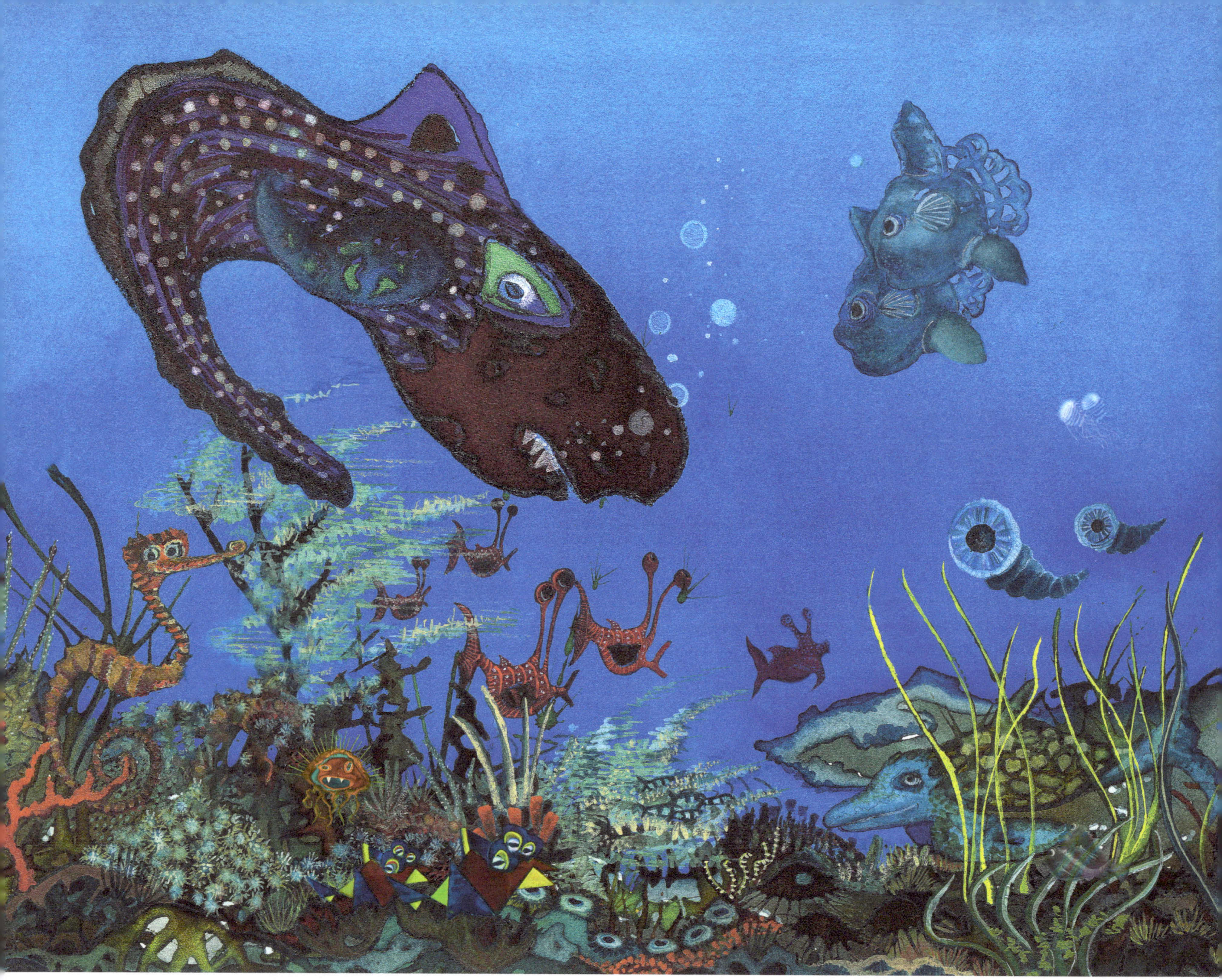

"Once, the ocean was filled with creatures of all shapes and sizes," said Grandpa.

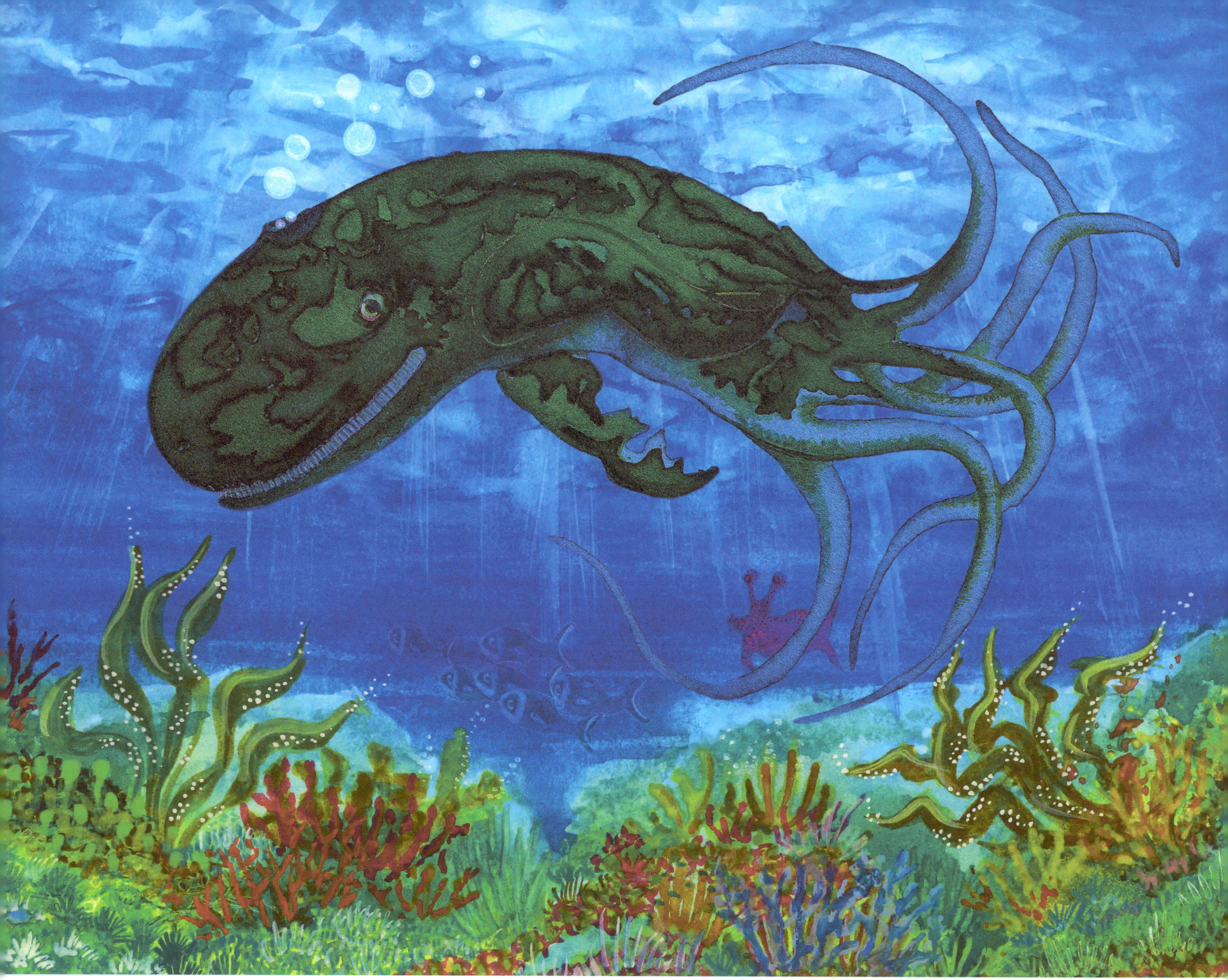

"The many-armed whallopus had a garden in the shade of a kelp forest and blew air from a hole in her head."

"The turtophin frolicked all day and crawled into her shell at night."

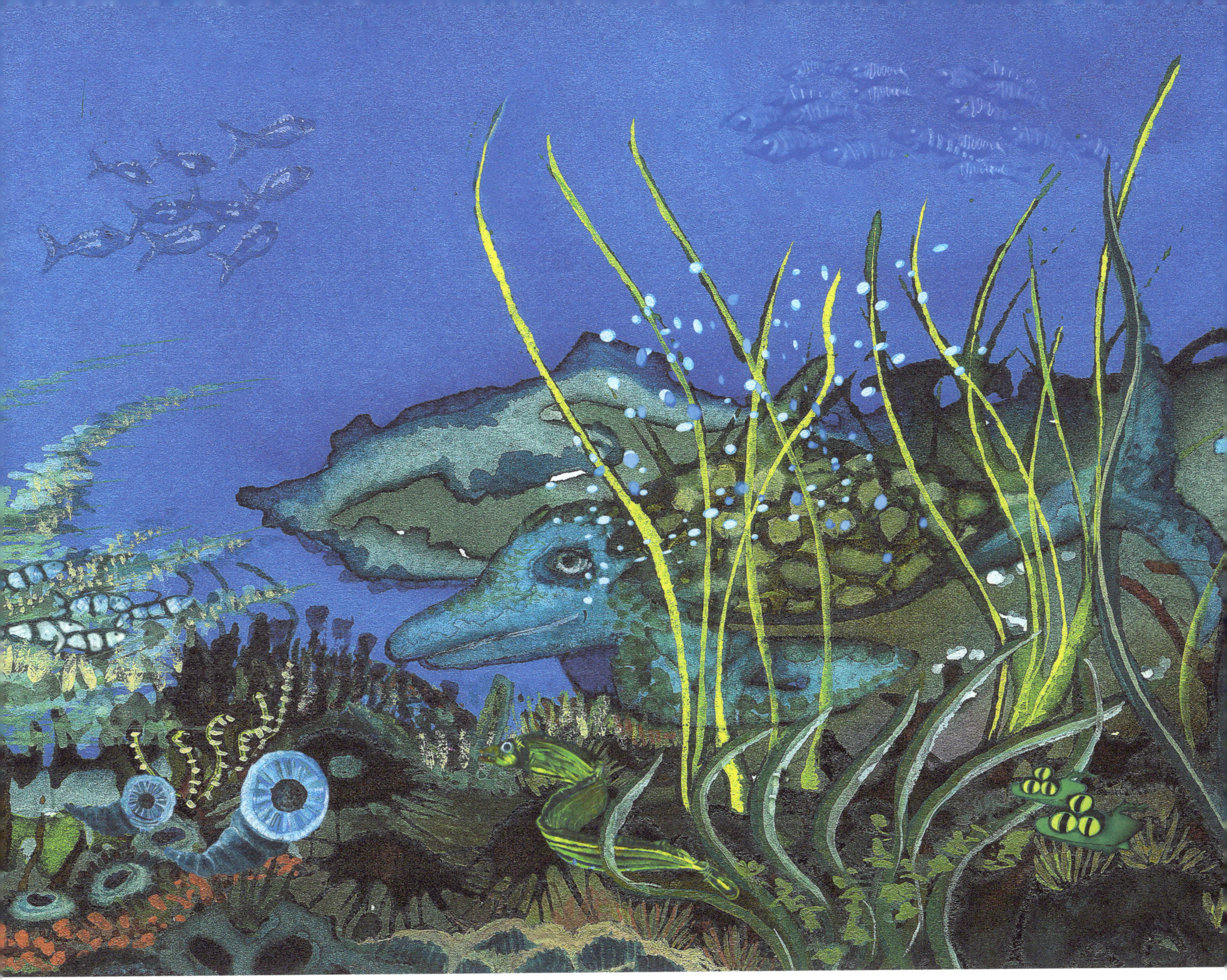

Sometimes, Grandpa's whallopus was an octowhally and the turtophins became dolphoturtles, but who knew? Not a jelliball now living had ever seen these creatures.

"But the most astounding of all were the medusae, which were color and light at the same time," Grandpa paused. The jelliballs held their breath.

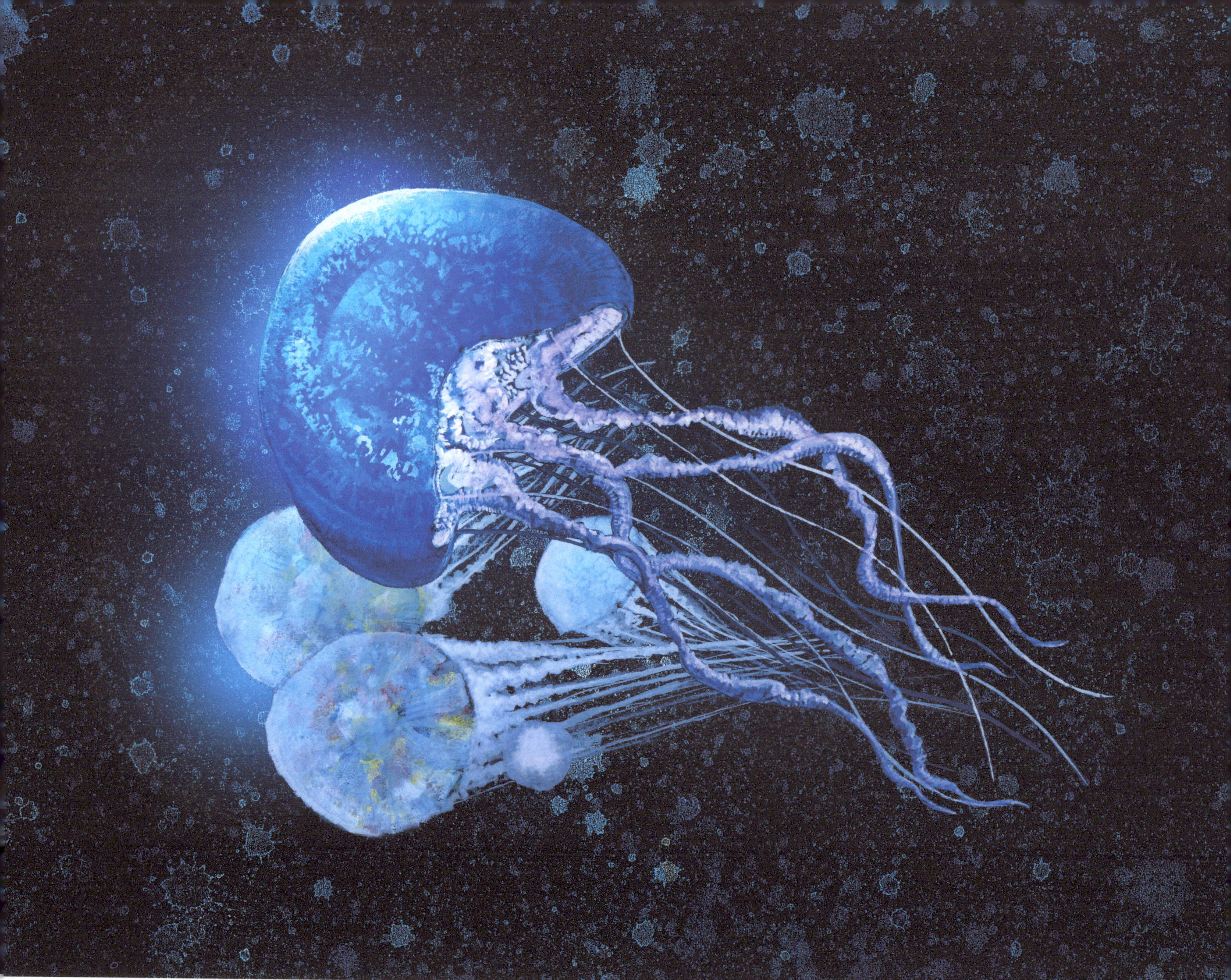

"They even glowed in the dark!"

Bobi tried very hard to imagine the bright light and the odd creatures. Could the ocean ever hold such marvelous things?

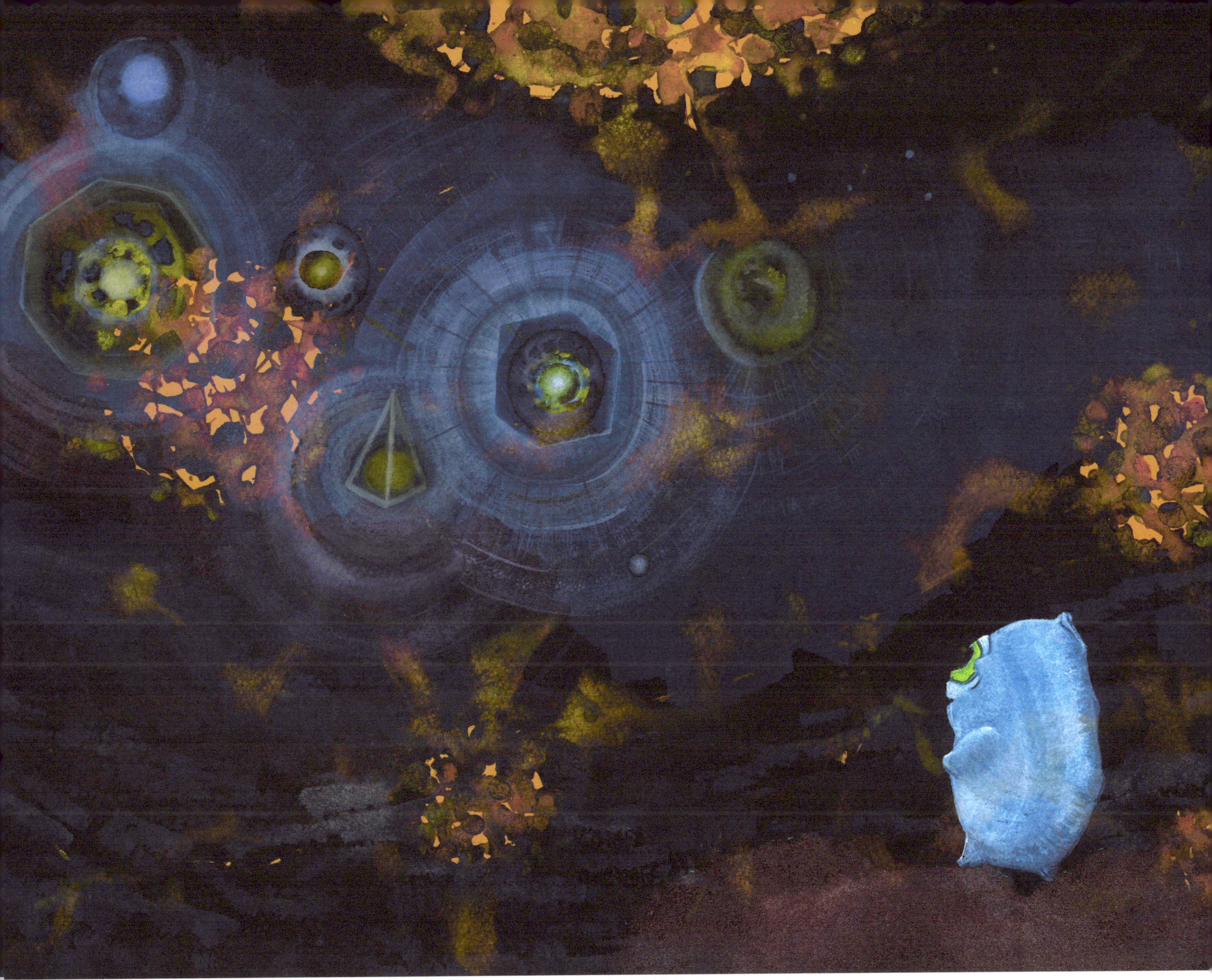

"Change came slowly," said Grandpa. "The fish elders harrumphed, blew stern bubbles out their nose and said, 'When I was young the water was so clear you could see for miles.'"

"The younger fish turned tail and didn't listen."

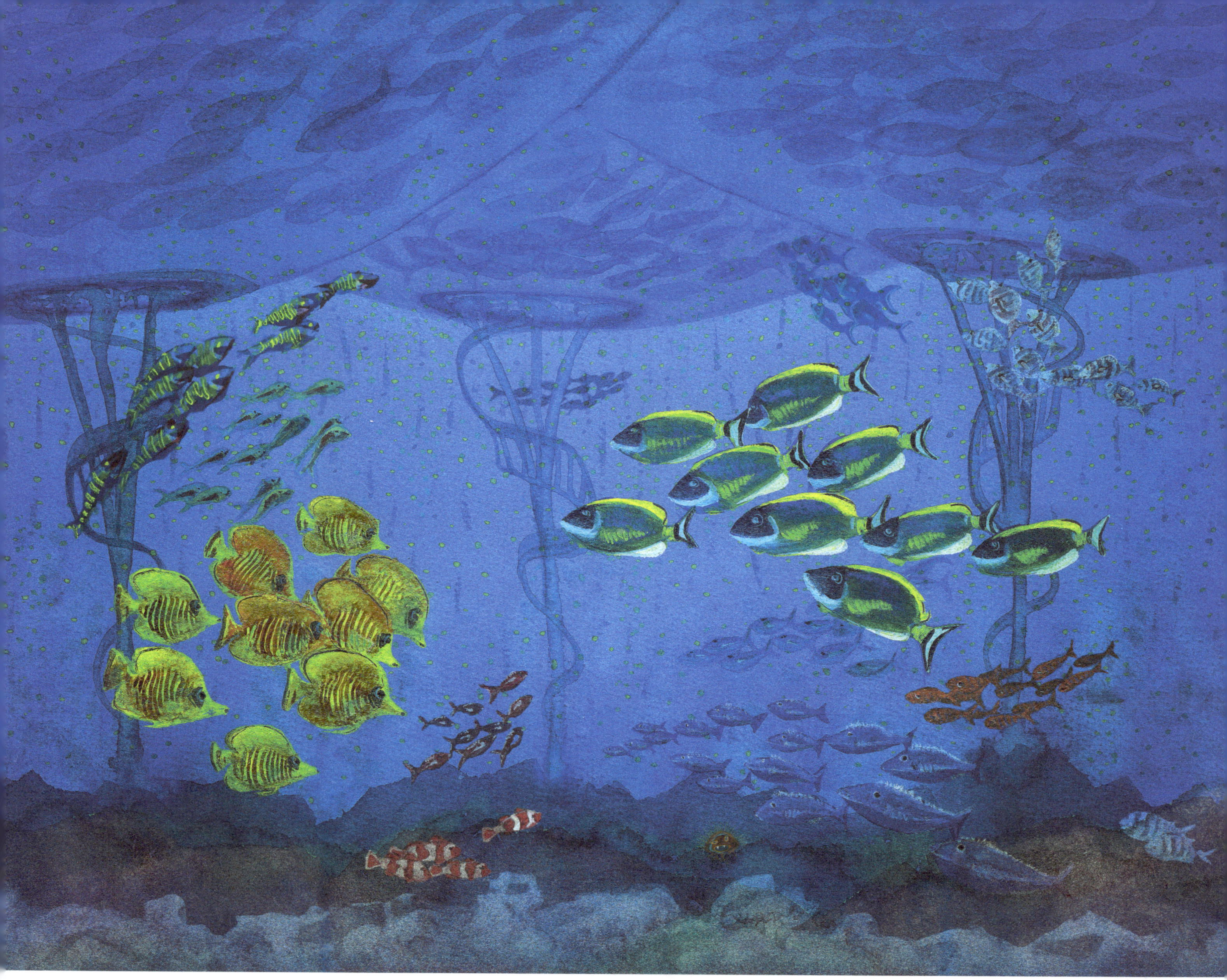

"Then, one by one, enormous cages appeared overhead. Food rained down at the same time every day," said Grandpa.

"Now, all the fish had to do was wait below with their mouths open. It was true there were thousands of fish crammed in the cages, but if you didn't swim too close and look into their sad eyes, you could almost forget they were there."

Bobi couldn't imagine the cages or the fish, but he knew what sad eyes looked like.

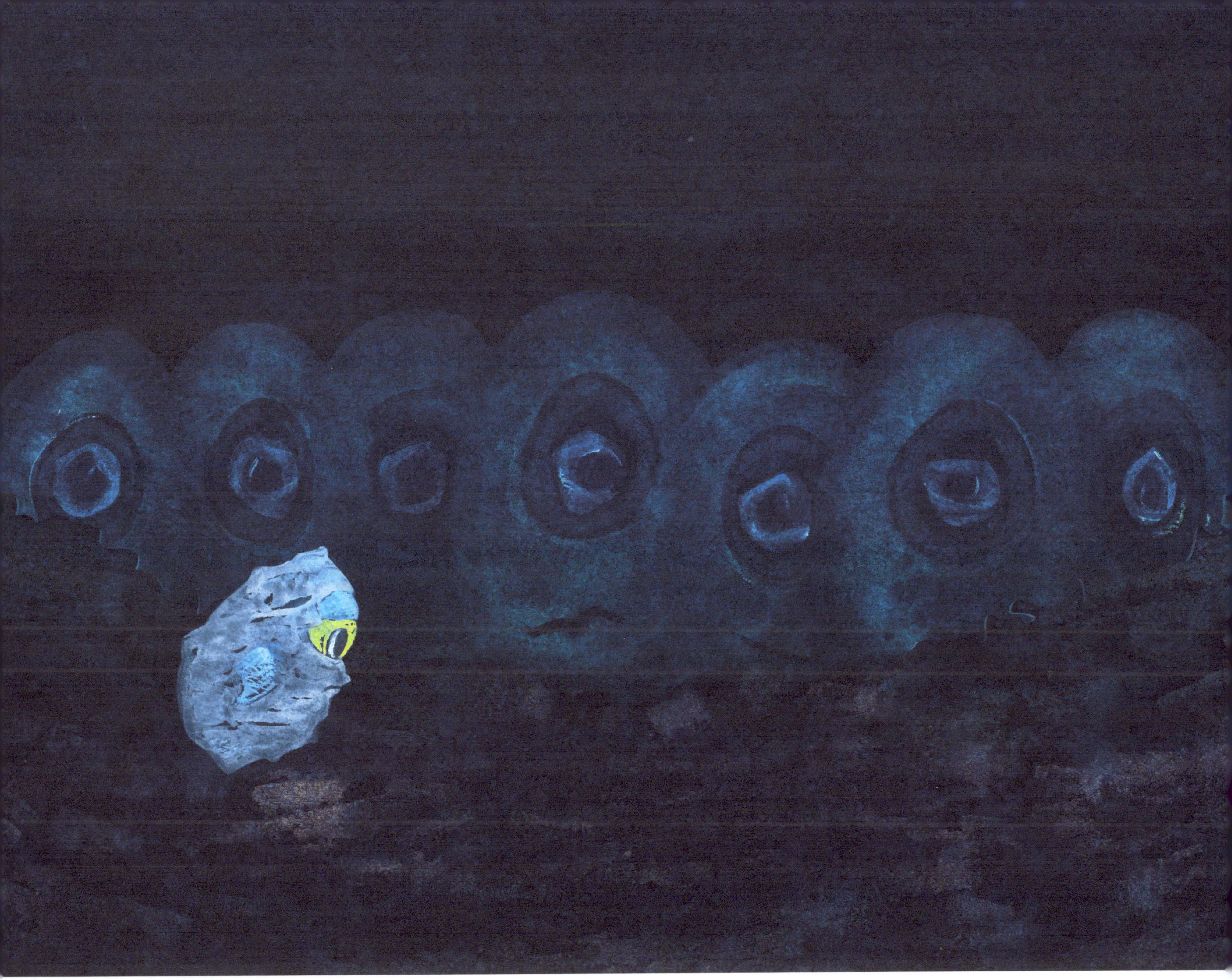

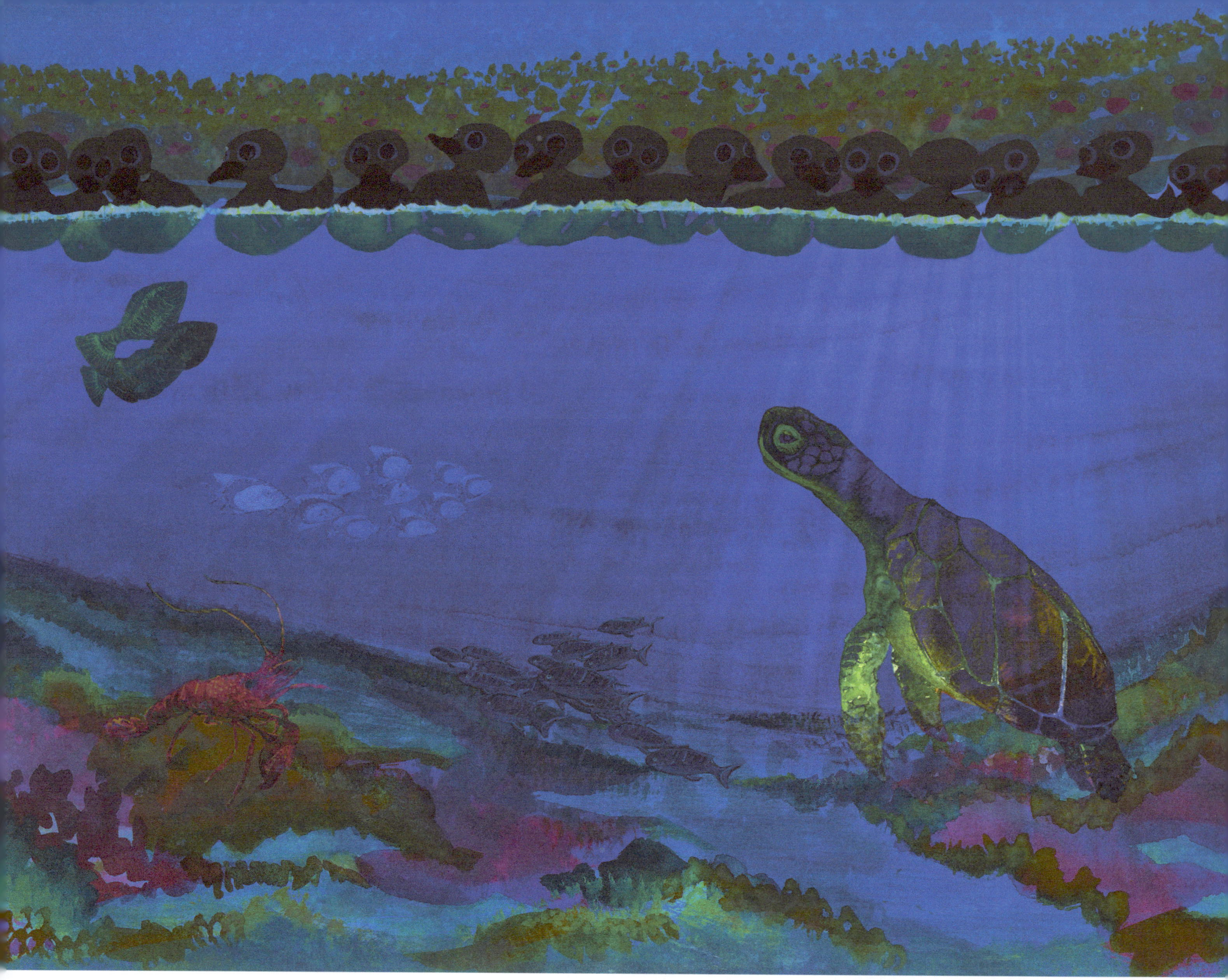

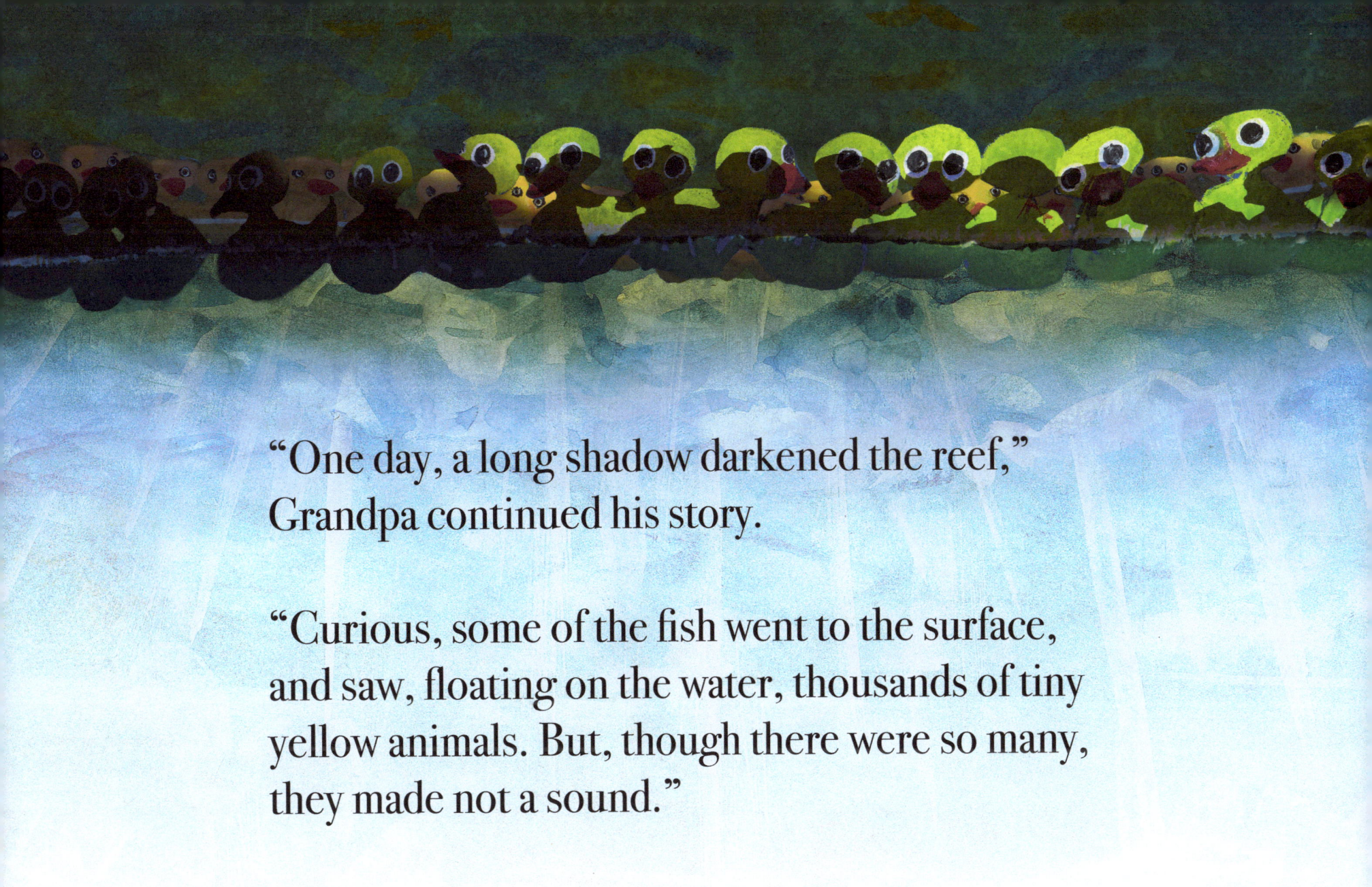

"One day, a long shadow darkened the reef," Grandpa continued his story.

"Curious, some of the fish went to the surface, and saw, floating on the water, thousands of tiny yellow animals. But, though there were so many, they made not a sound."

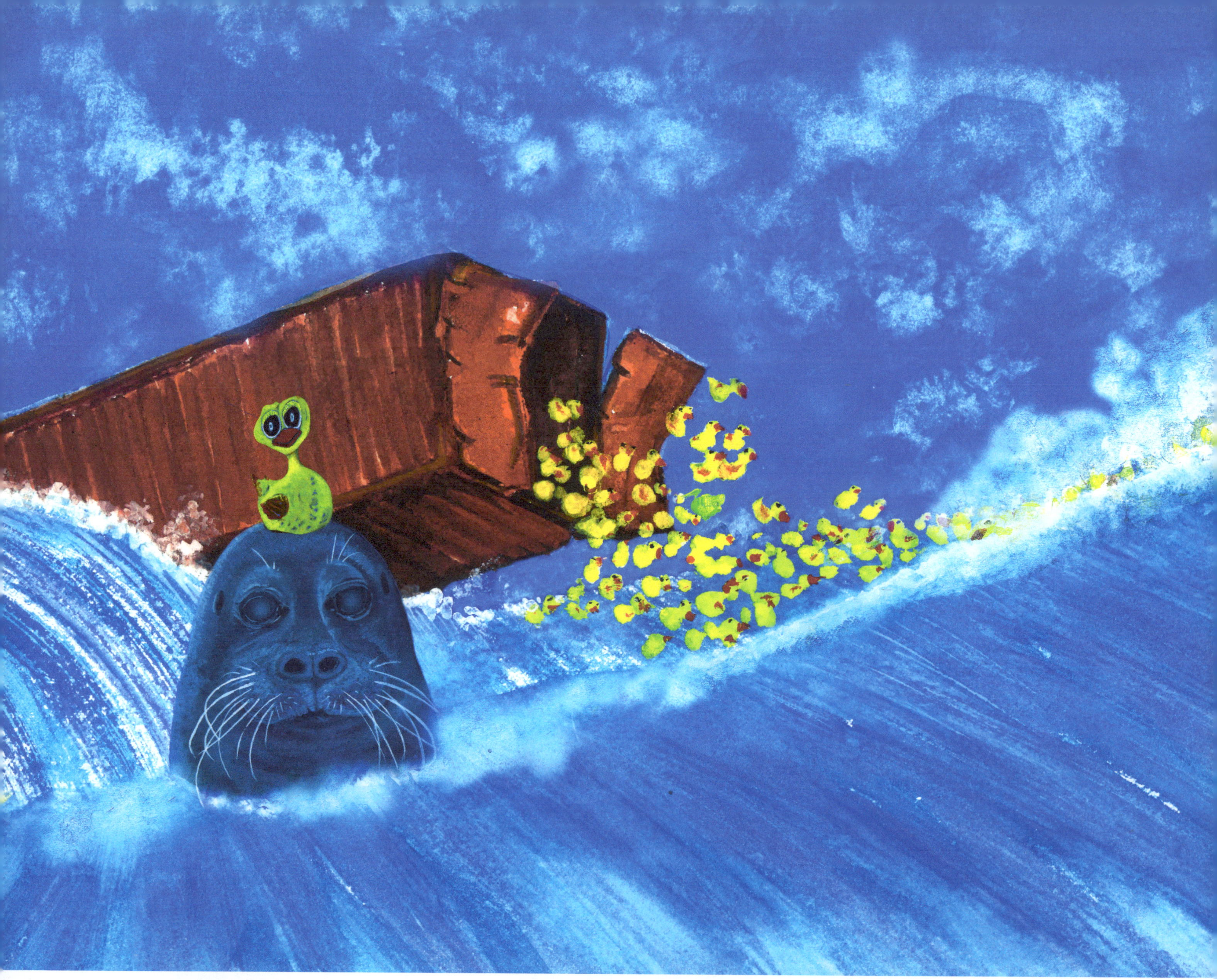

"Just then a sharkarruda bit down on one of the animals. 'Quack!' it protested."

Grandpa made a funny quacking sound.
Bobi and the jellies laughed and jiggled.

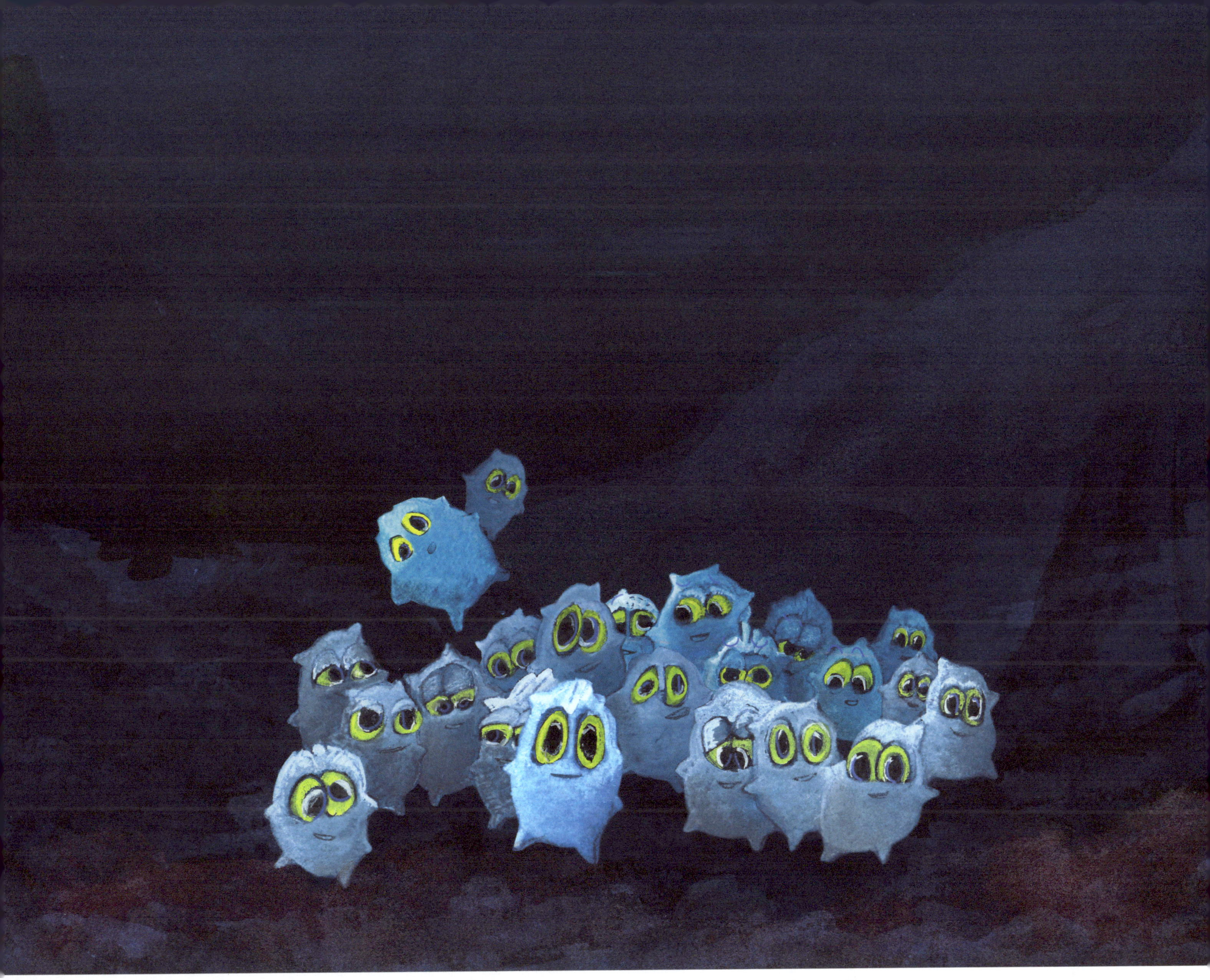

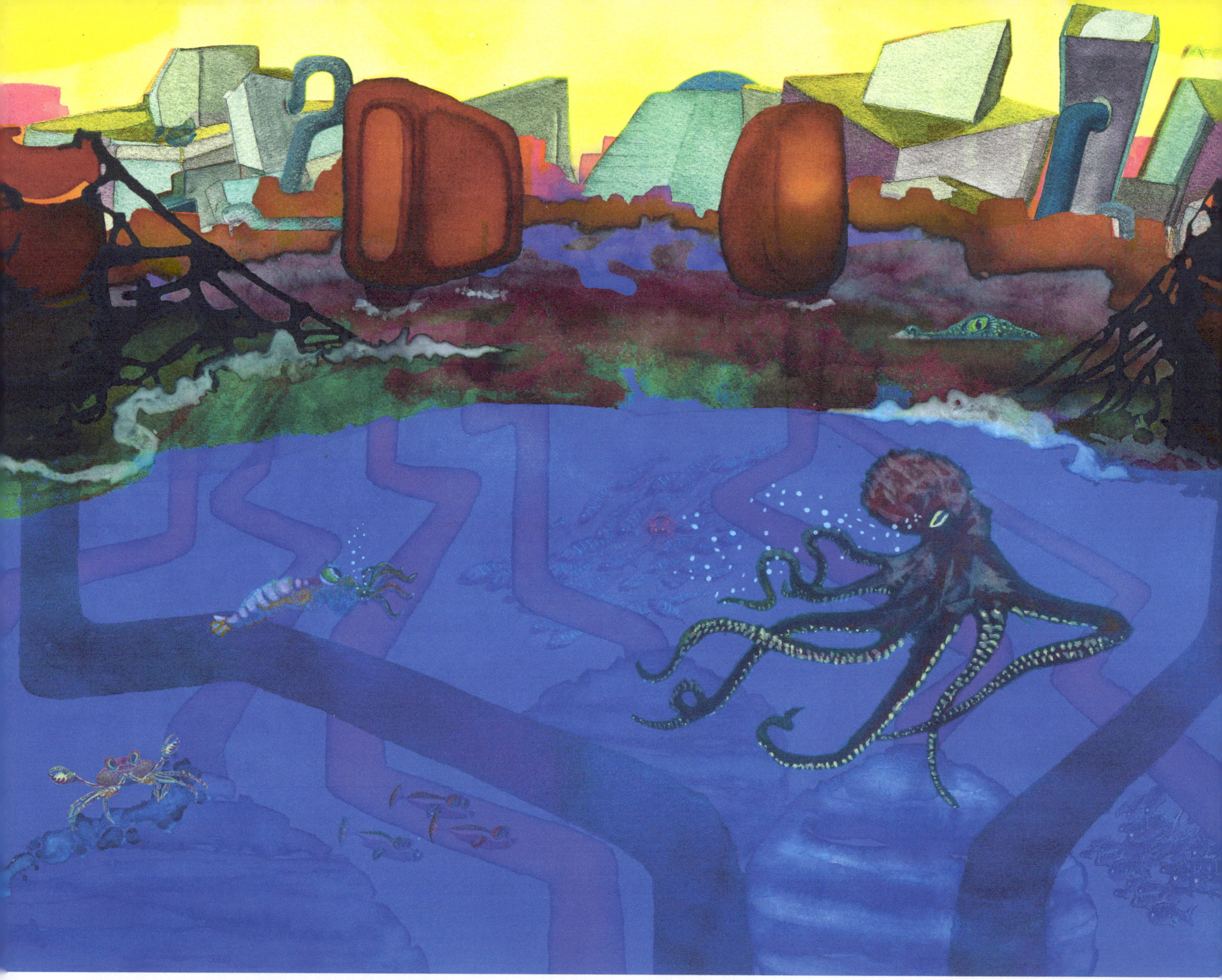

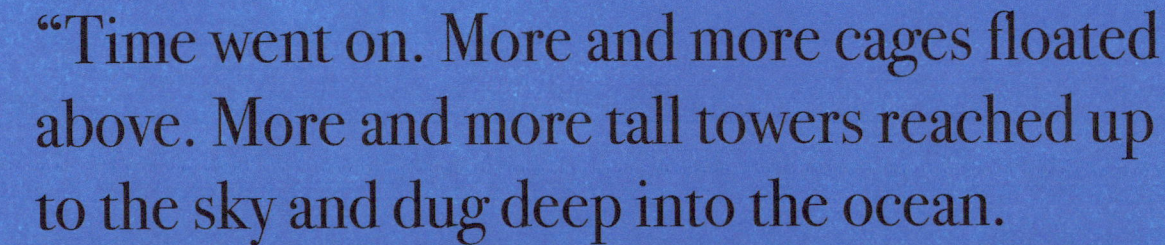

"Time went on. More and more cages floated above. More and more tall towers reached up to the sky and dug deep into the ocean. Sometimes, dark sticky goop floated around these towers. Birds got it on their wings and couldn't fly."

"So many things fell into the water," said Grandpa, "they left no room for the fish."

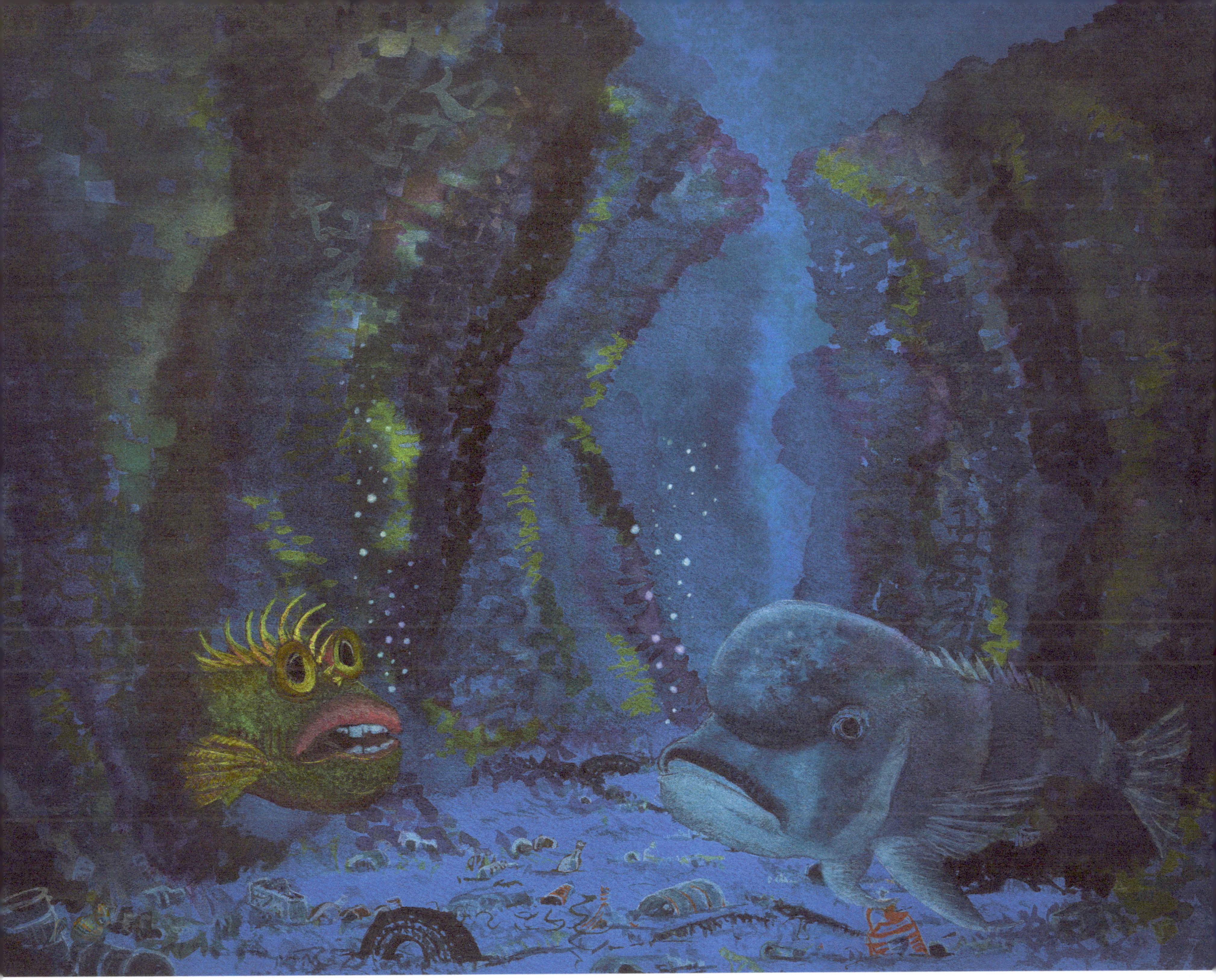

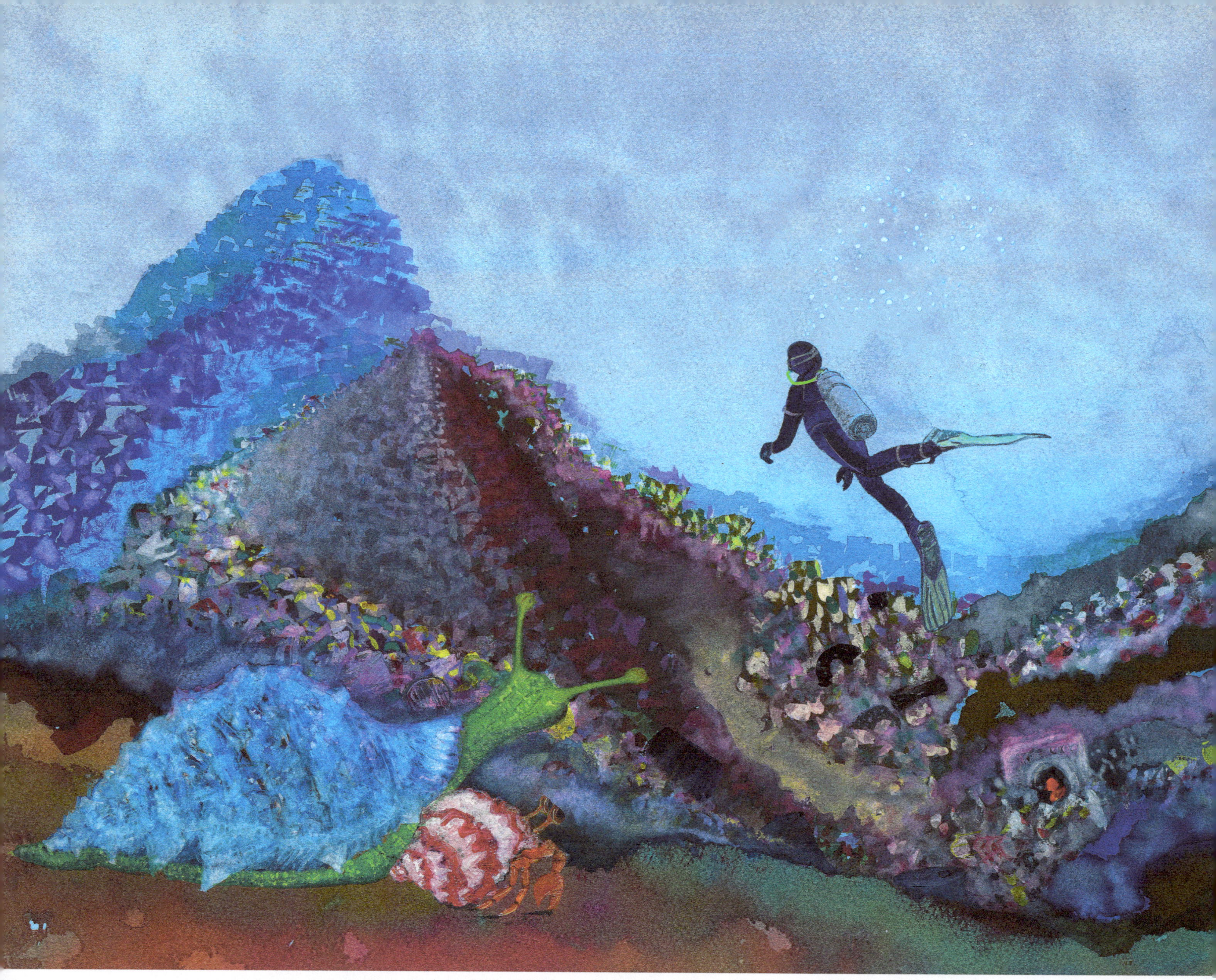

"Even those creatures with funny round things on their faces stopped visiting the reef. They blew bubbles and beat their two long tentacles to swim back to the surface."

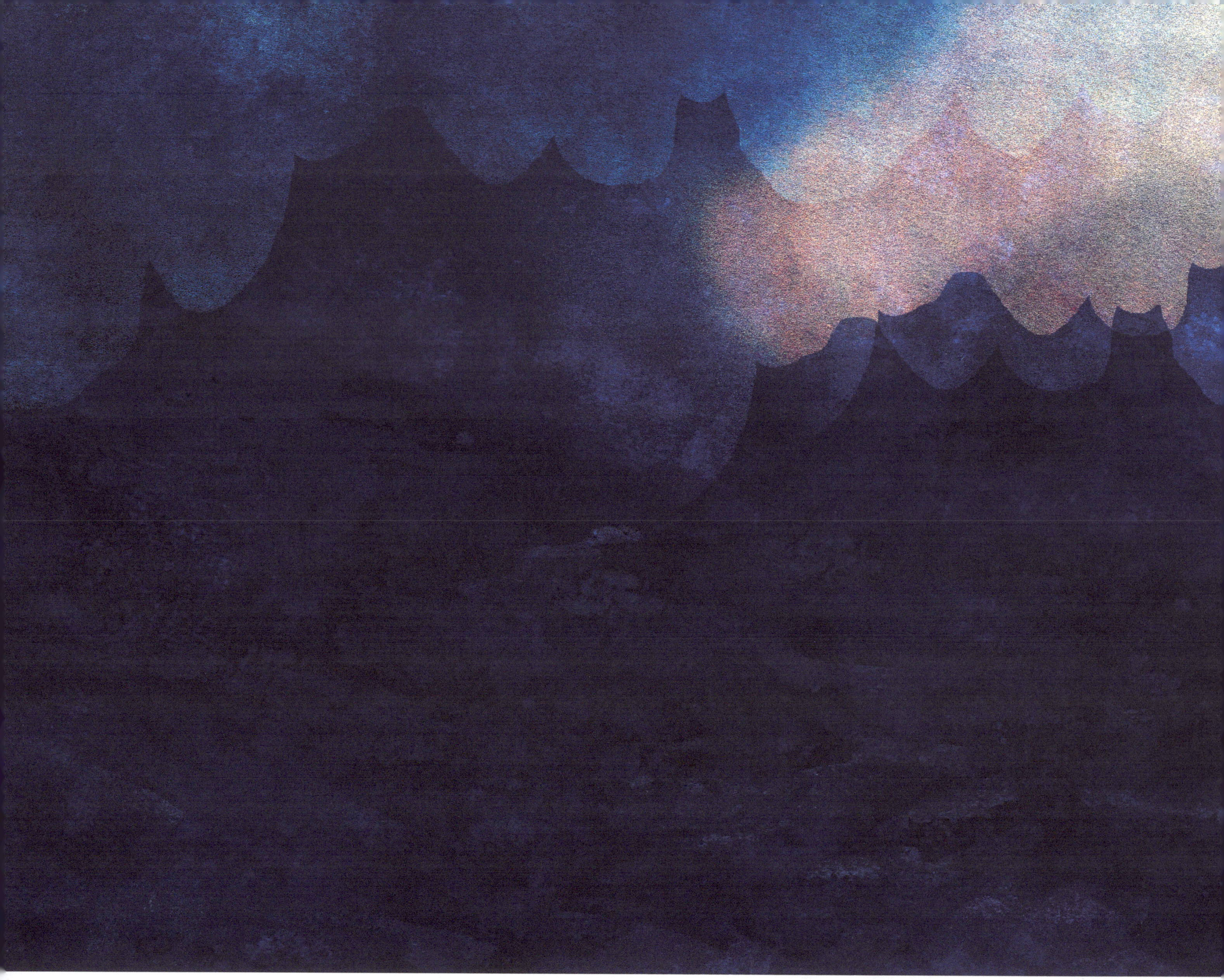

The surface, Bobi knew, was somewhere above, very, very far away. He wanted to go there some day.

"The medusae stopped glowing."

"The beautiful, multicolored coral turned to crumbling white skeletons."

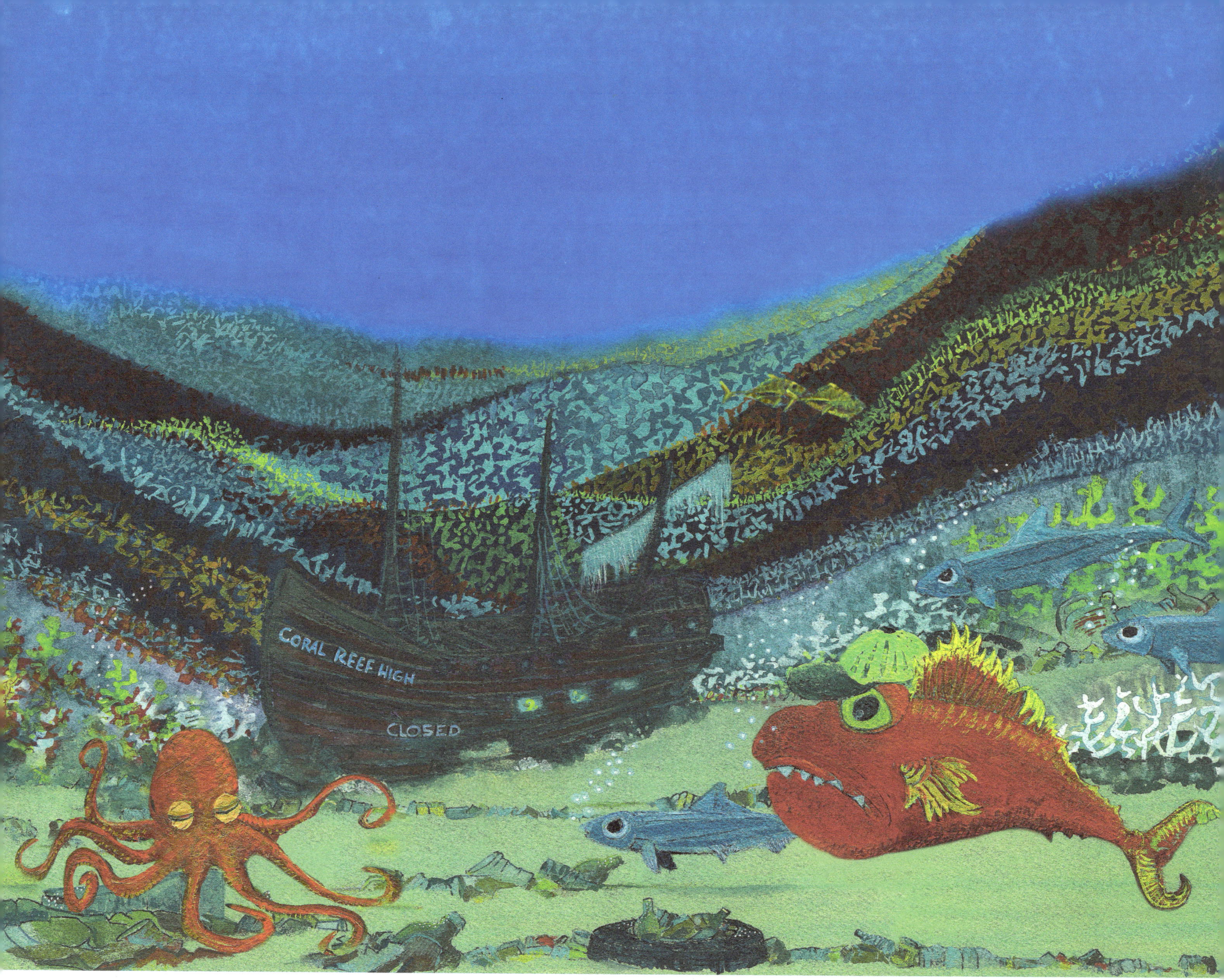
CORAL REEF HIGH
CLOSED

"Fish stopped going to school," said Grandpa. Bobi and his friends smiled. They liked the idea of not going to school.

"Derformed creatures moved sluggishly through the murky water. And still more garbage fell into the sea until it could hold no more."

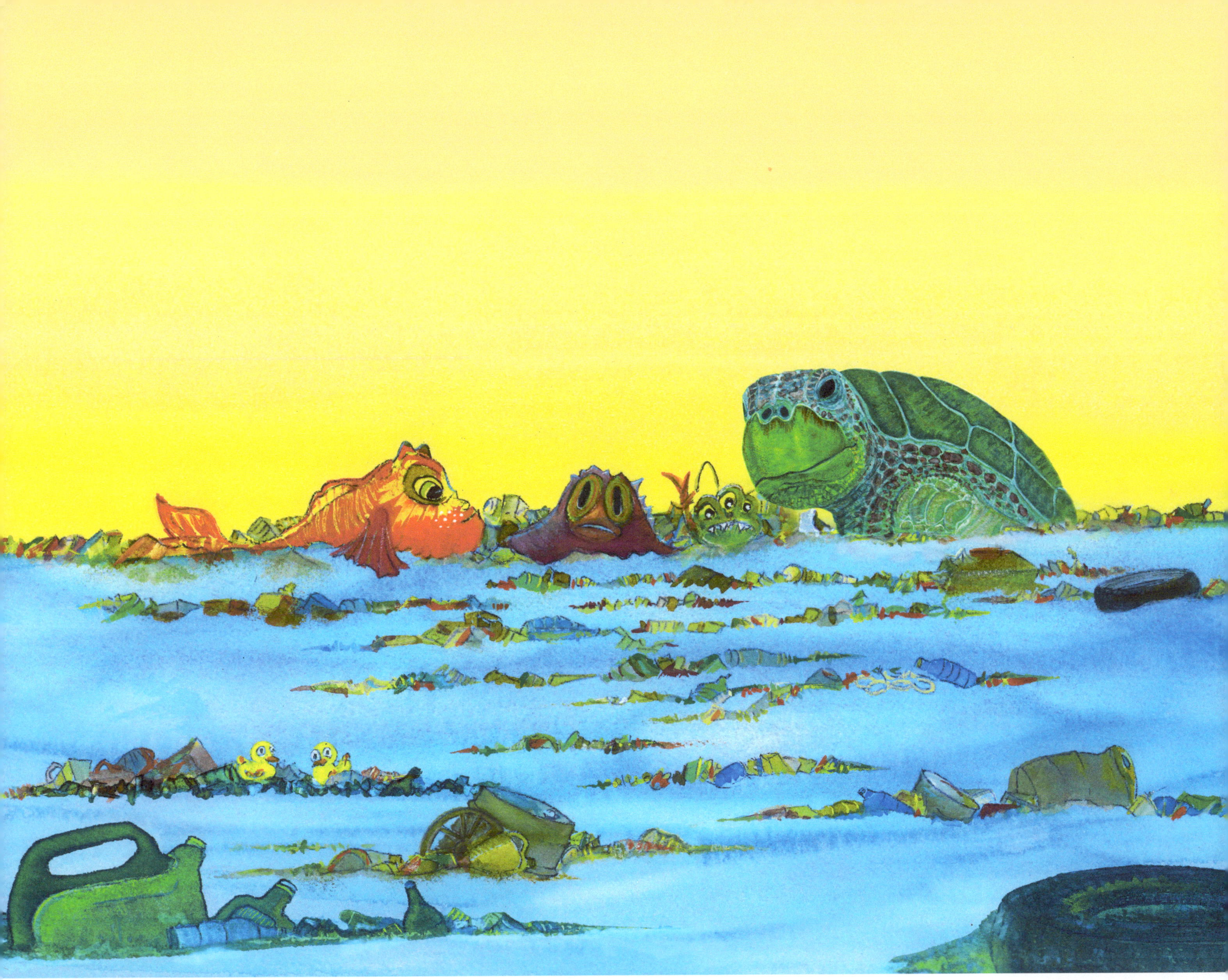

"One day the angry earth shuddered like a dogfish shaking off fleas."

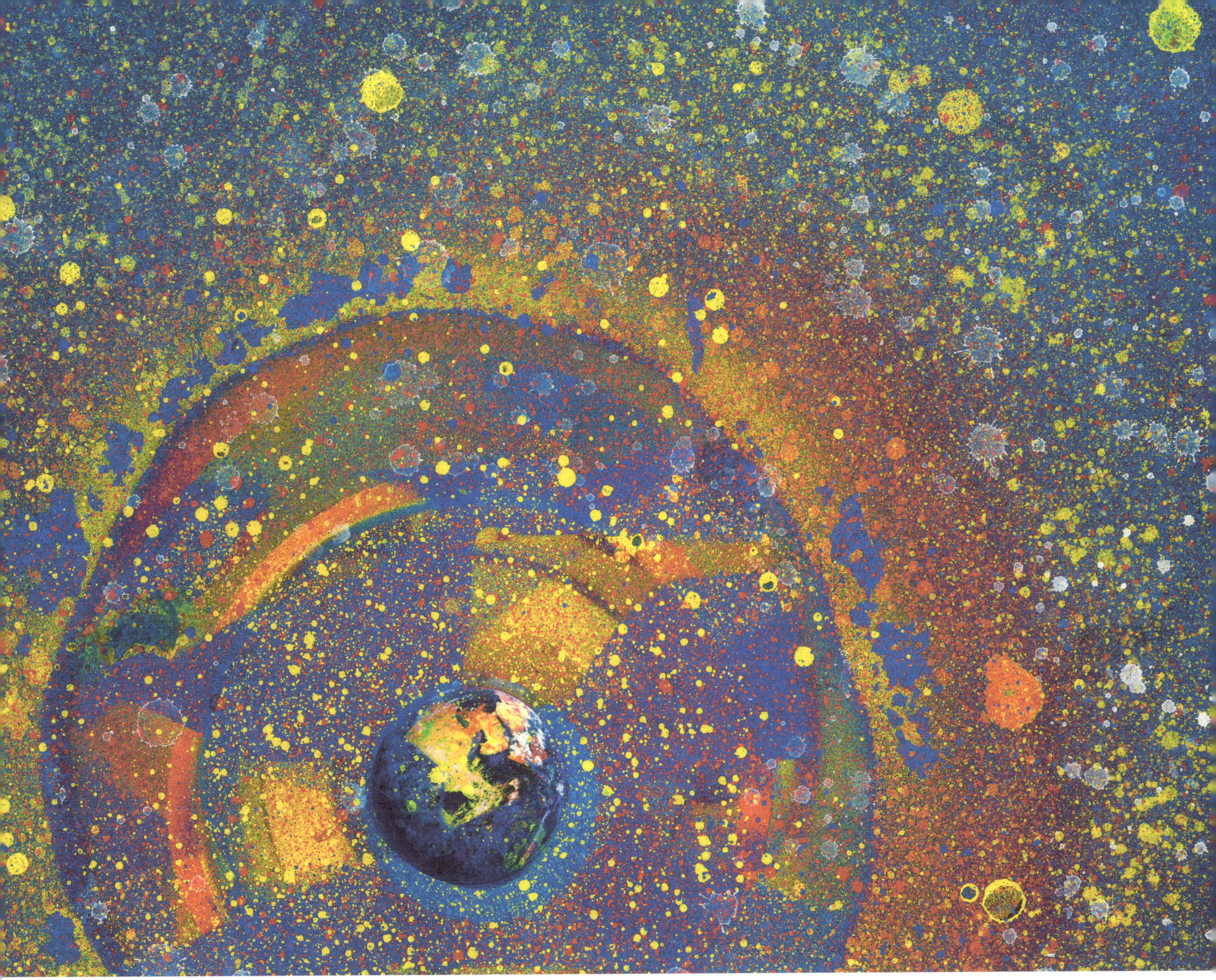

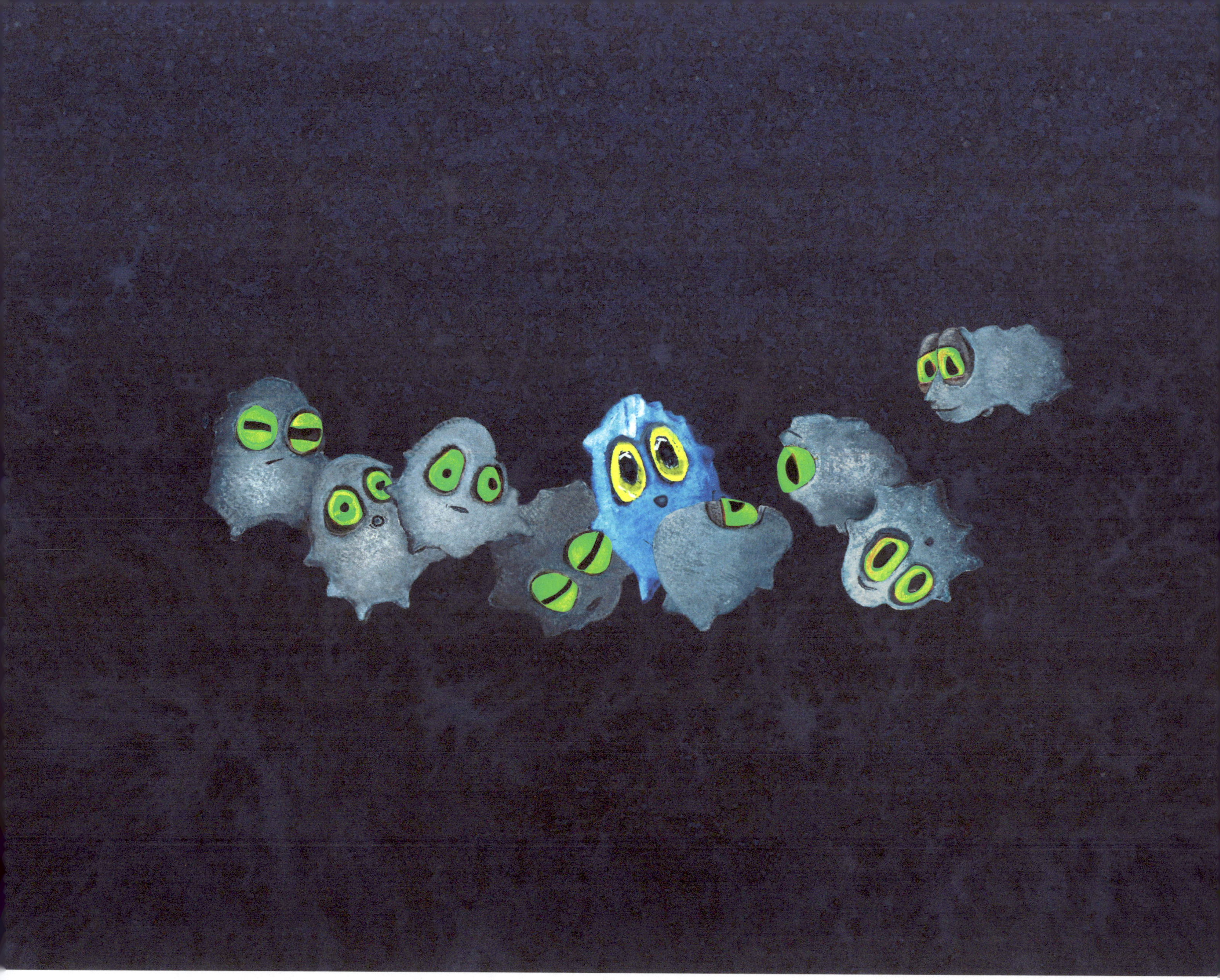

The jellies shuddered, too. This was the scariest part of Grandpa's story.

"The last of the jelliballs sought safety under submerged mountains and down dizzying canyons so deep that the brightest sunlight could never penetrate the darkness."

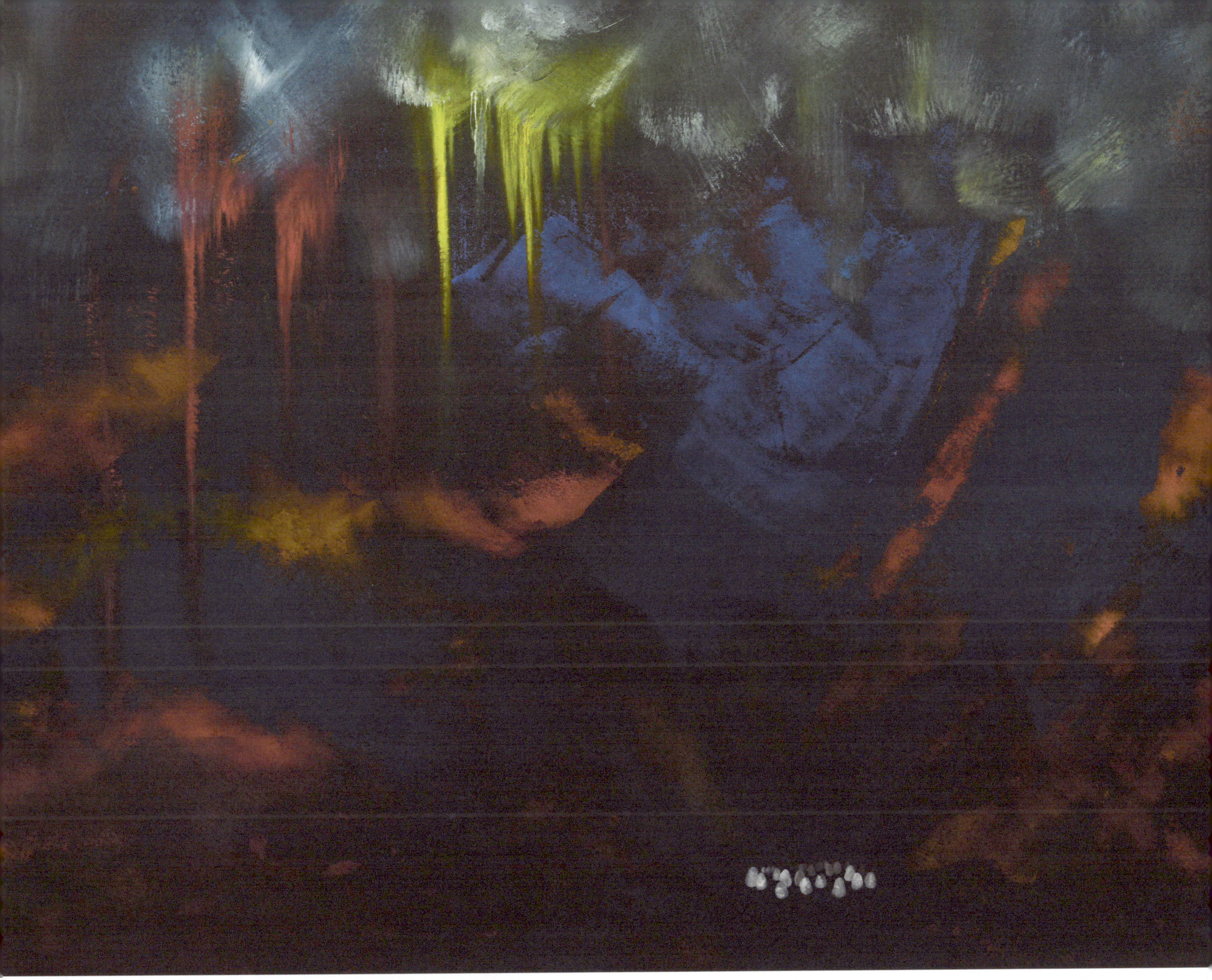

"And here, in an ocean eerie and still, we have lived for more years than we can count on all of our tentacles." Grandpa finished his story.

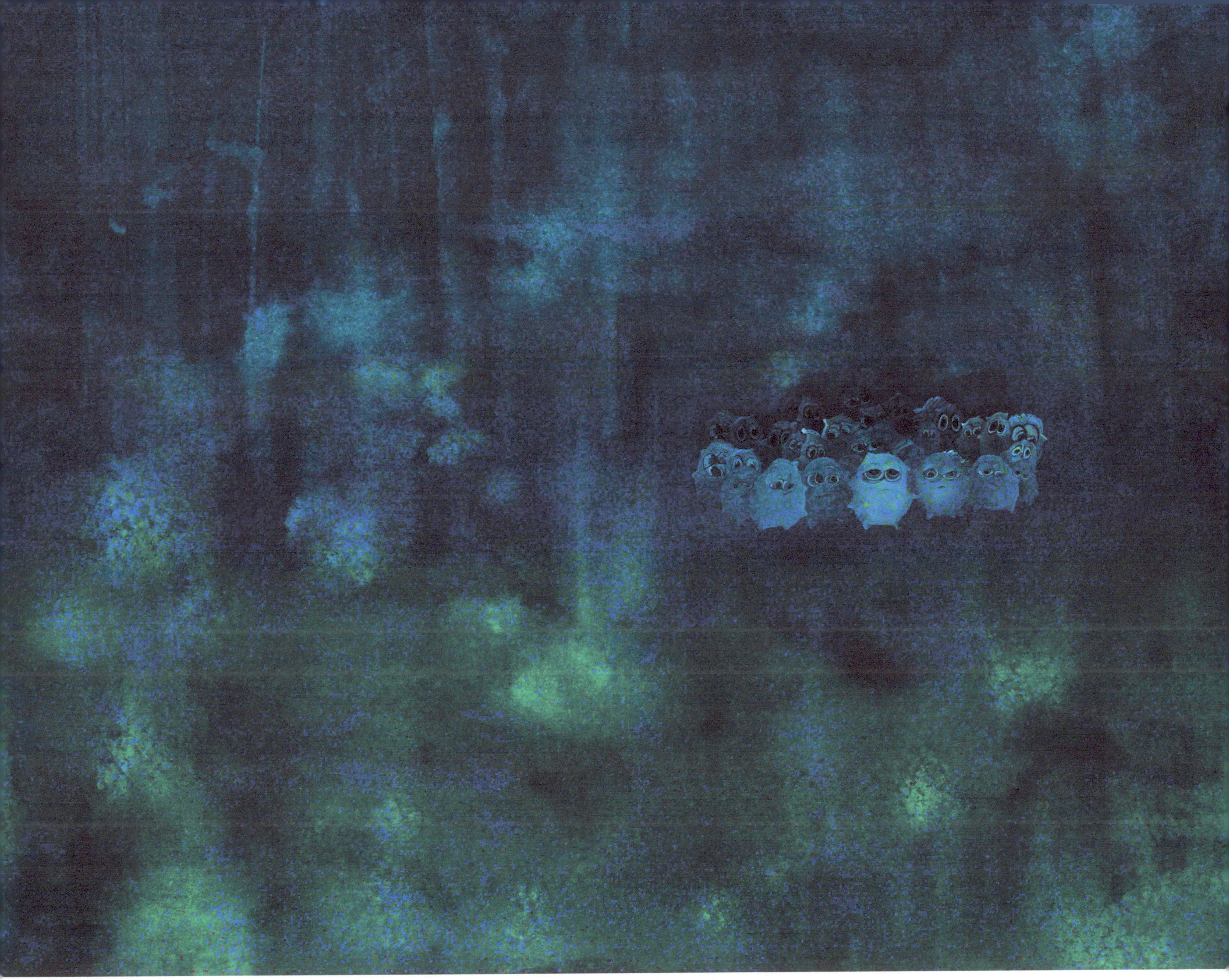

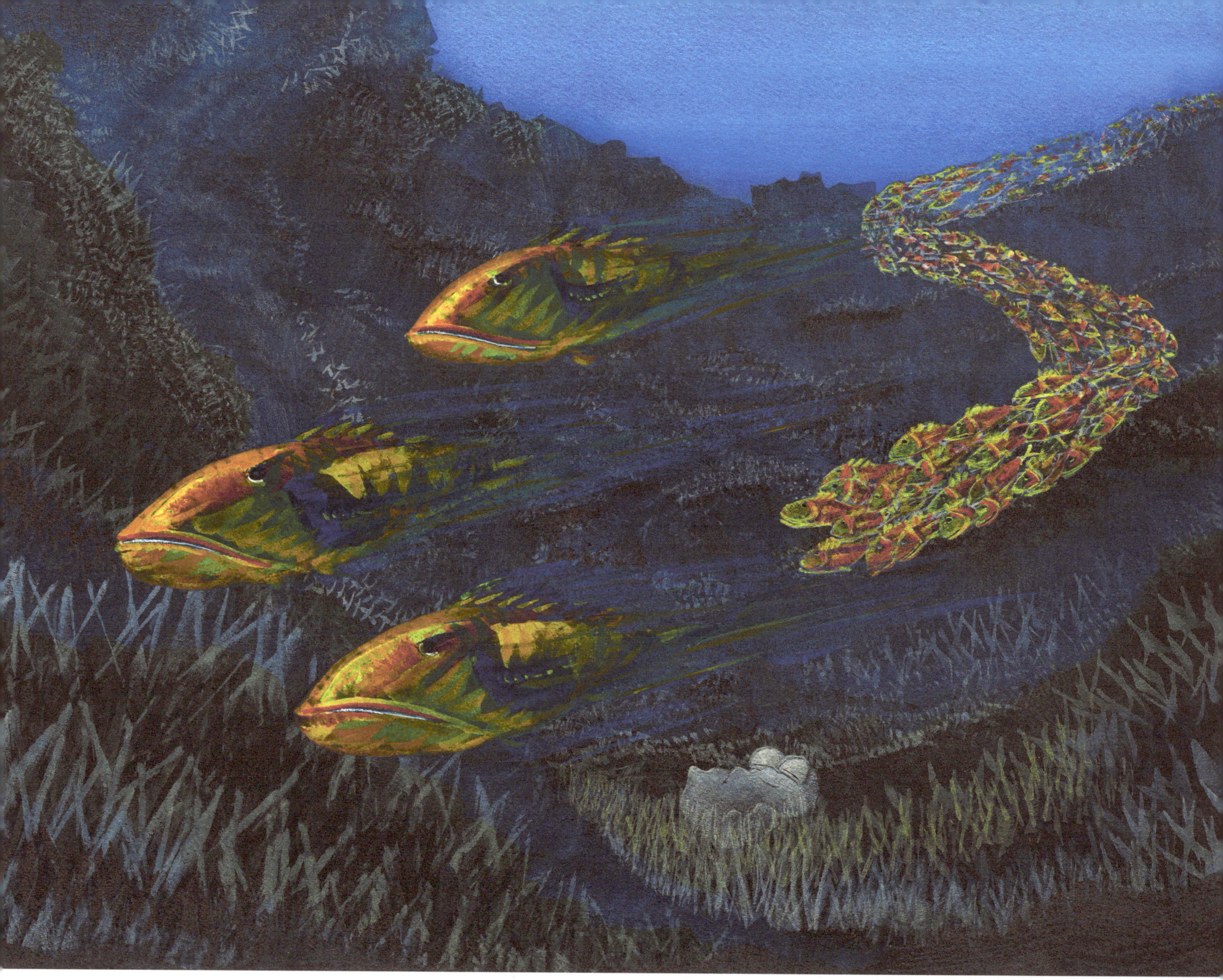

That night brightly colored fish darted in and out of the corners of Bobi's dreams.

A giant medusa filled every inch of his imagination.
In his sleep, he struggled to swim after the fish.

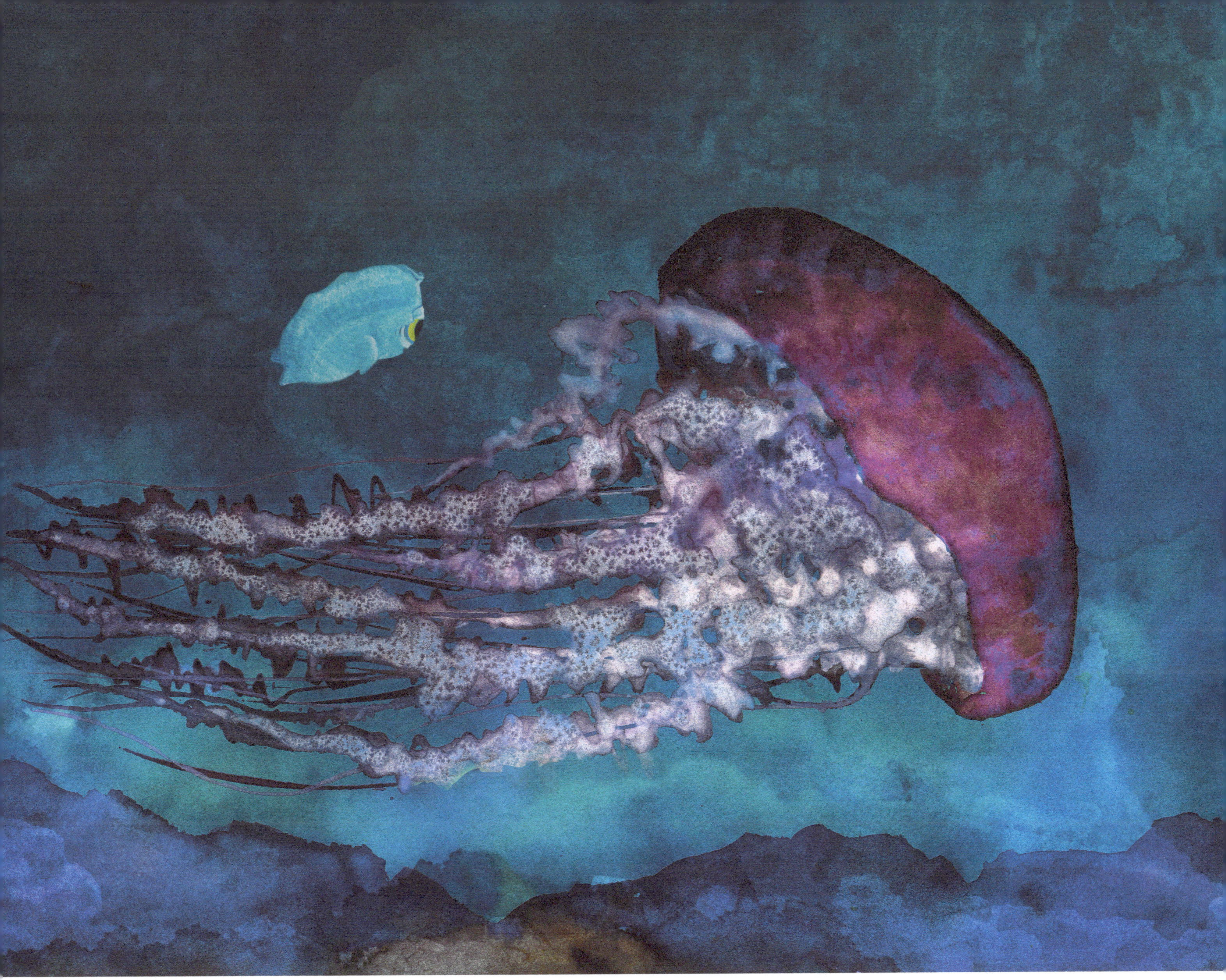

Bobi woke with a start. "Today I'm going to swim!"
But how would he do it?

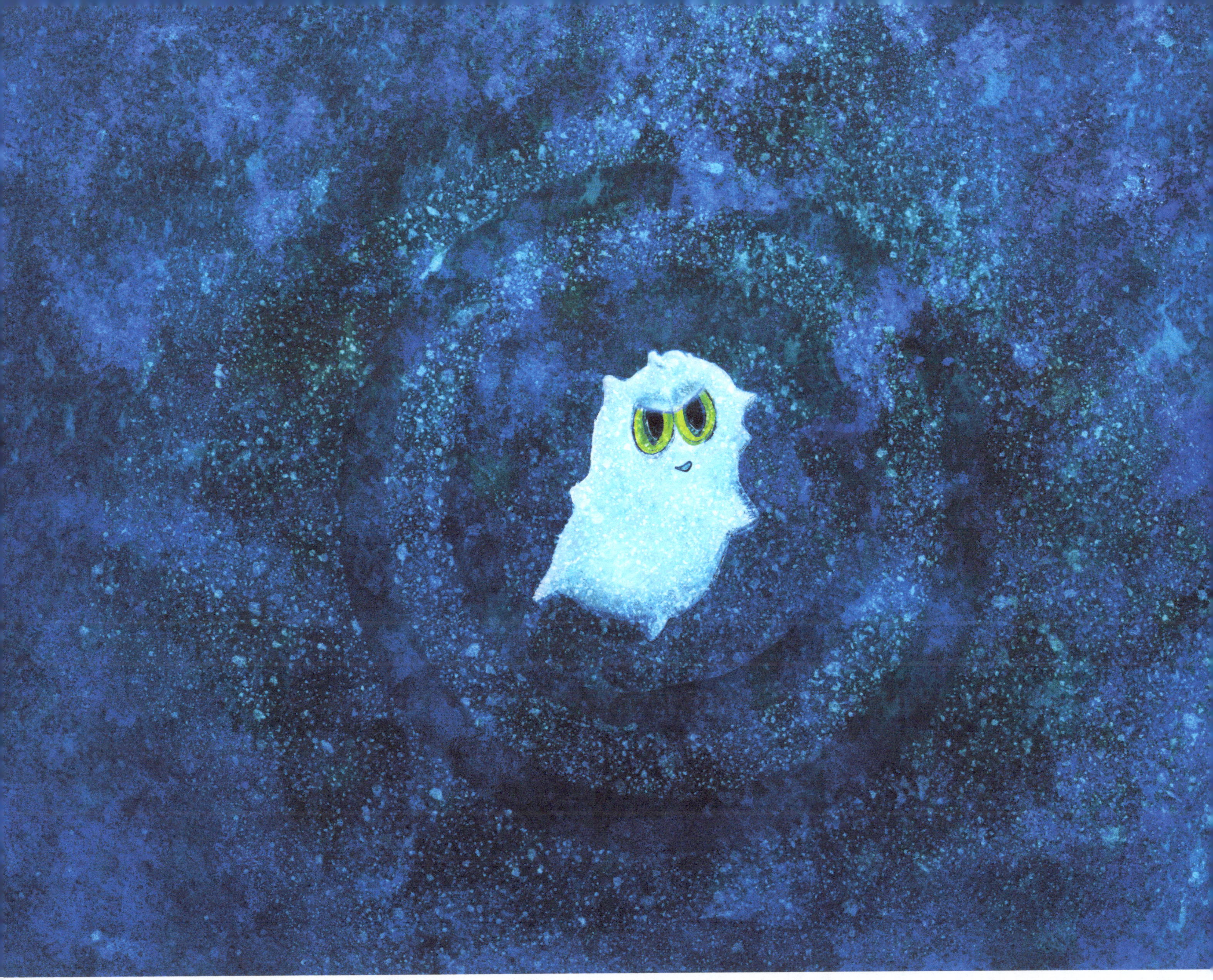

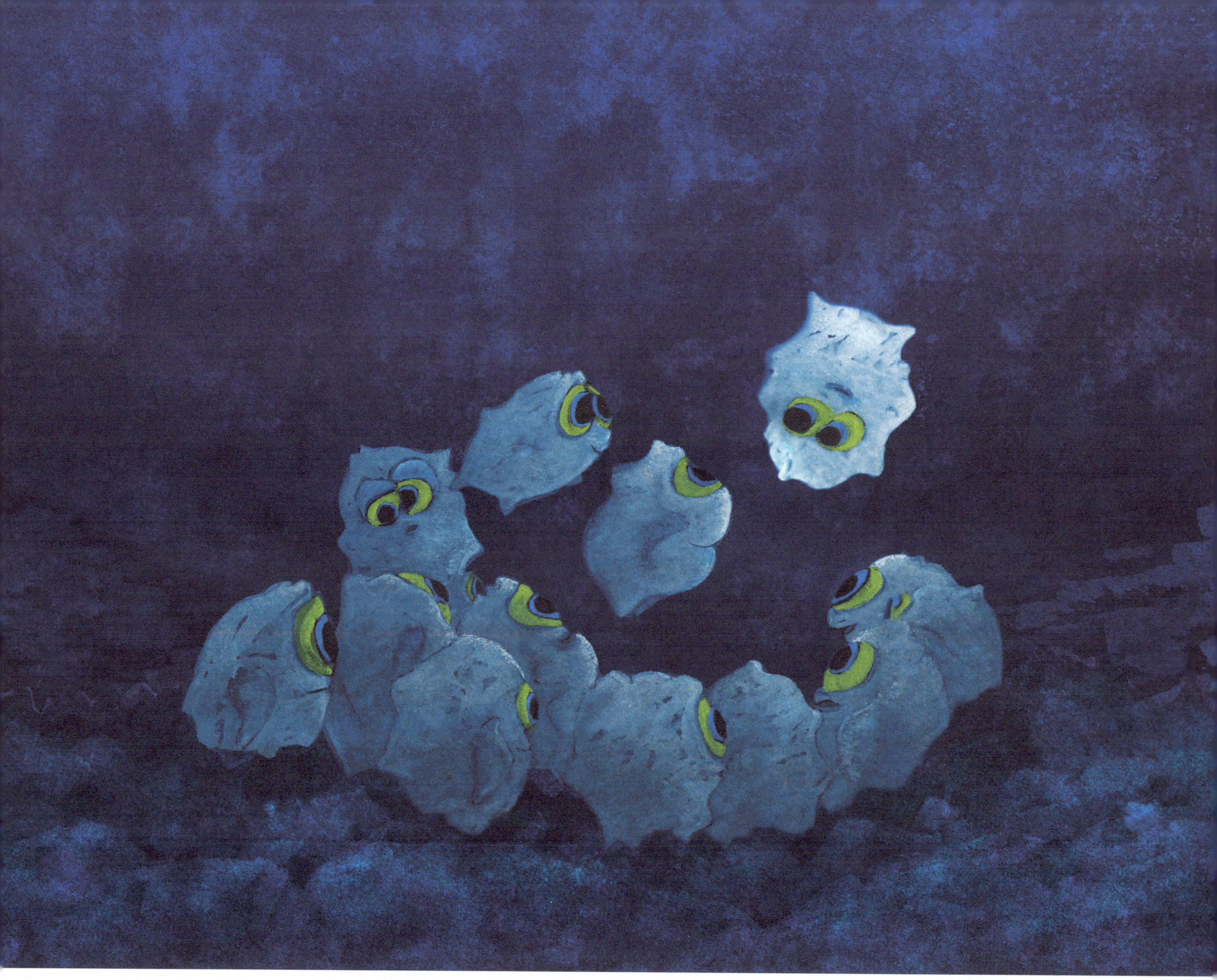

Bobi and his friends had round jiggly bodies, with tentacles on the sides and at the bottom. These tentacles sat at opposite angles. And that was the problem. When the left tentacles wanted to go in one direction, the right pulled the other way.

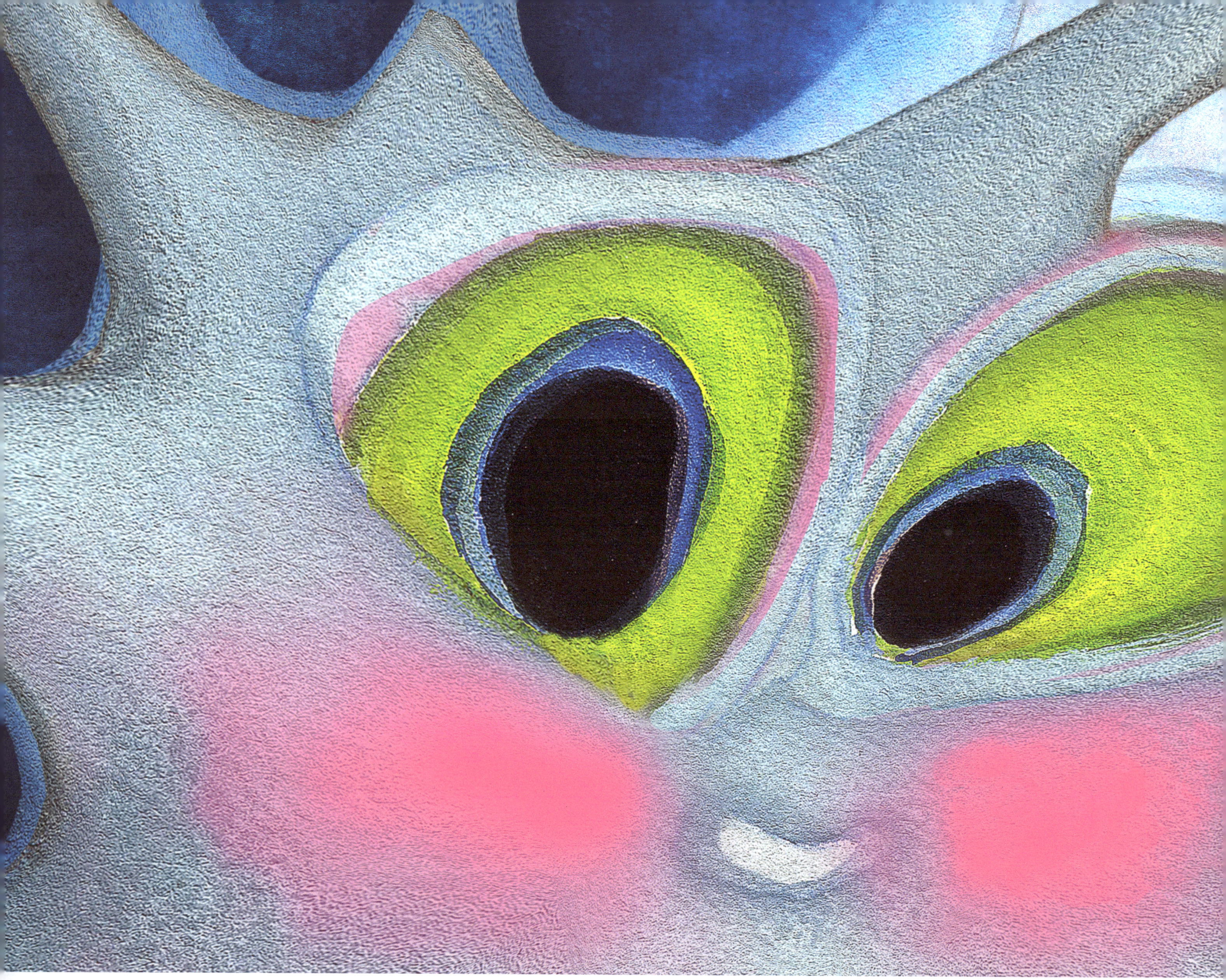

But Bobi was determined to swim! He made a stubborn, scrunched-up face. His right tentacles pulled to the right, his left tentacles pulled to the left. His body stretched a little. He pulled so hard he turned pink. "Stop!" his friends cried. "You'll hurt yourself!"

In a mighty tug of war, he pulled further and further and further apart. And just when it seemed he could stretch no more, he snapped back together with a huge sucking sound that flattened his body and left his tentacles dangling at his sides.

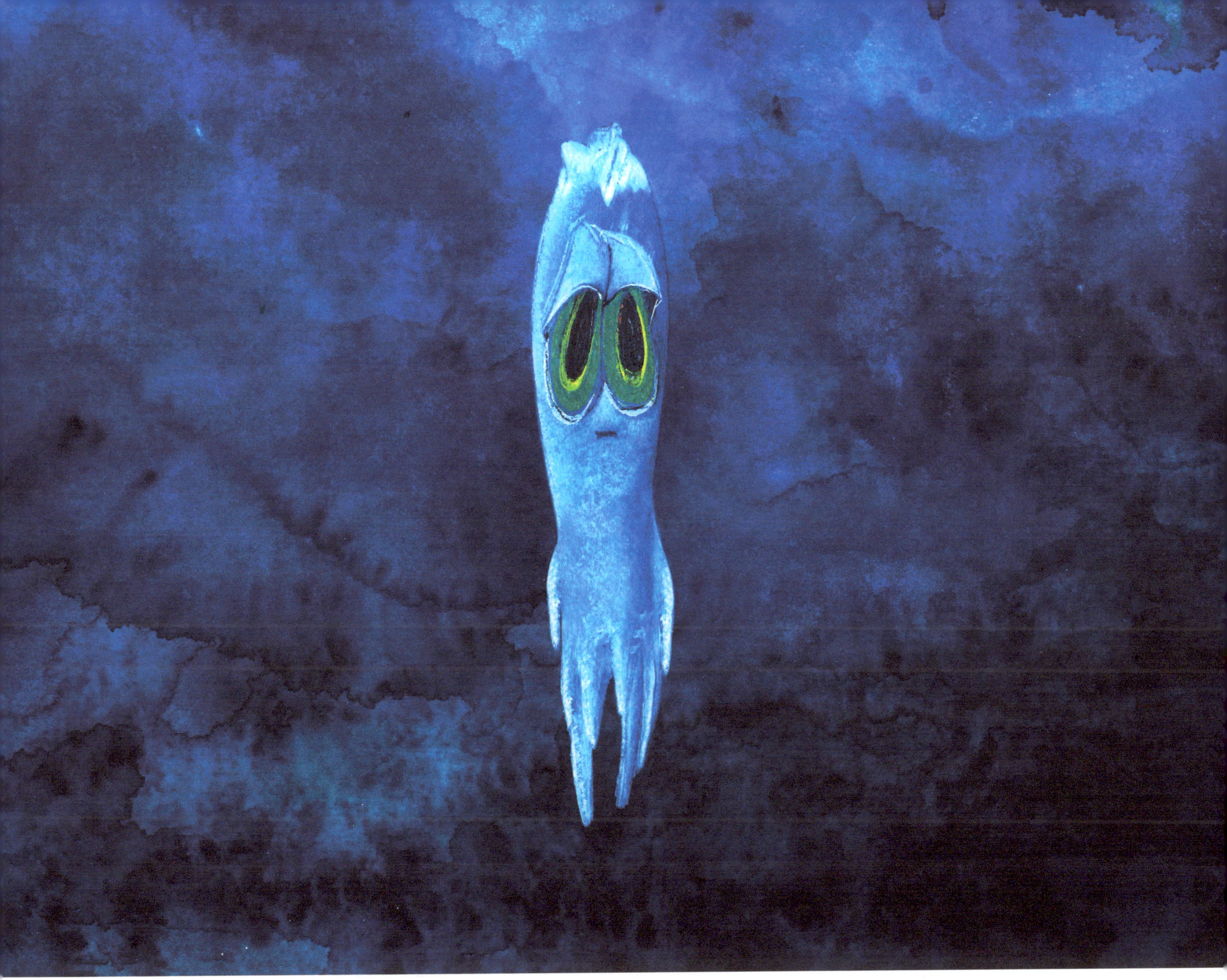

He wriggled a little and slid forward.

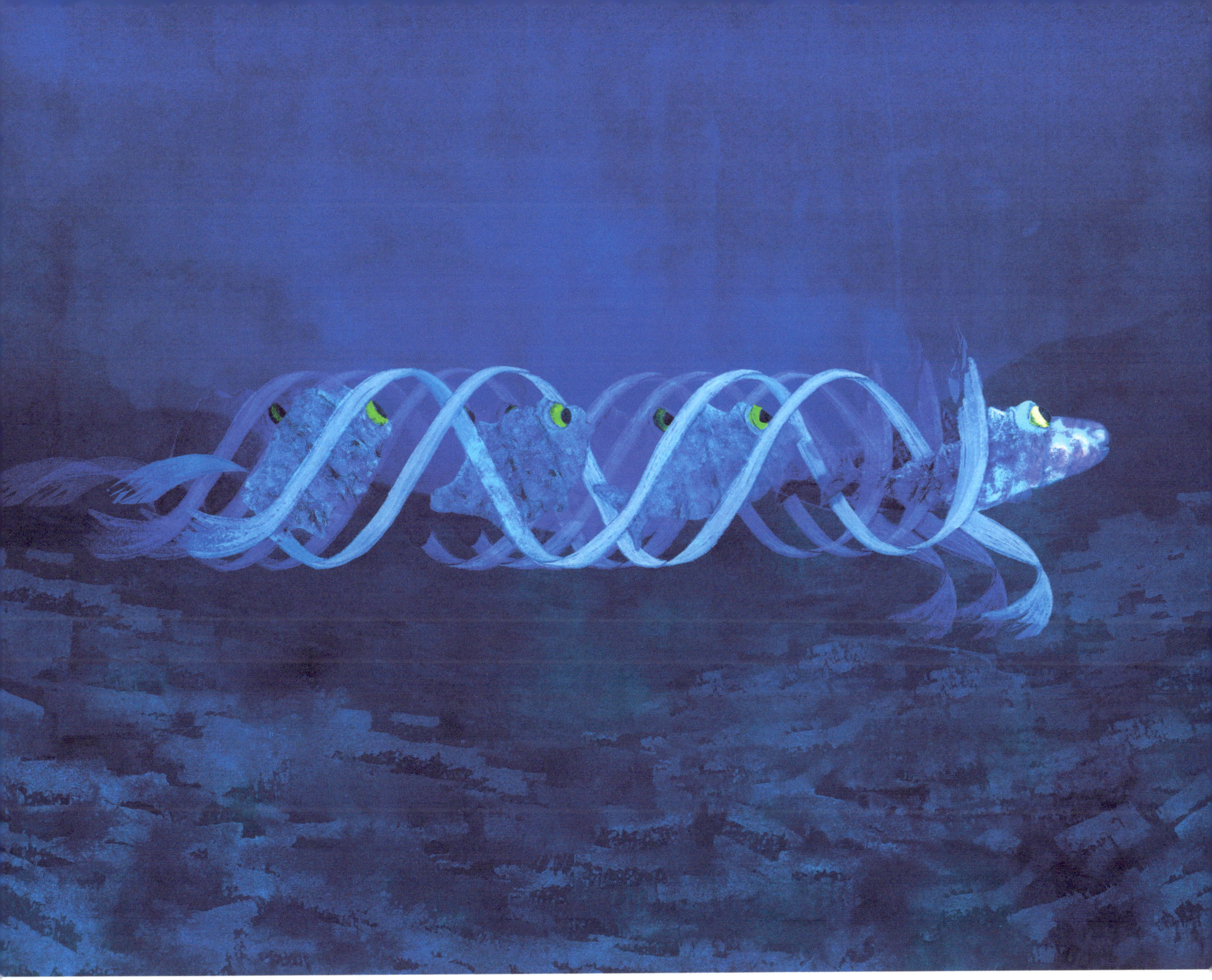

He took a turn around his friends.
He flicked his new tail and fluttered
his new fins in delight.
"Look! Bobi's swimming!"

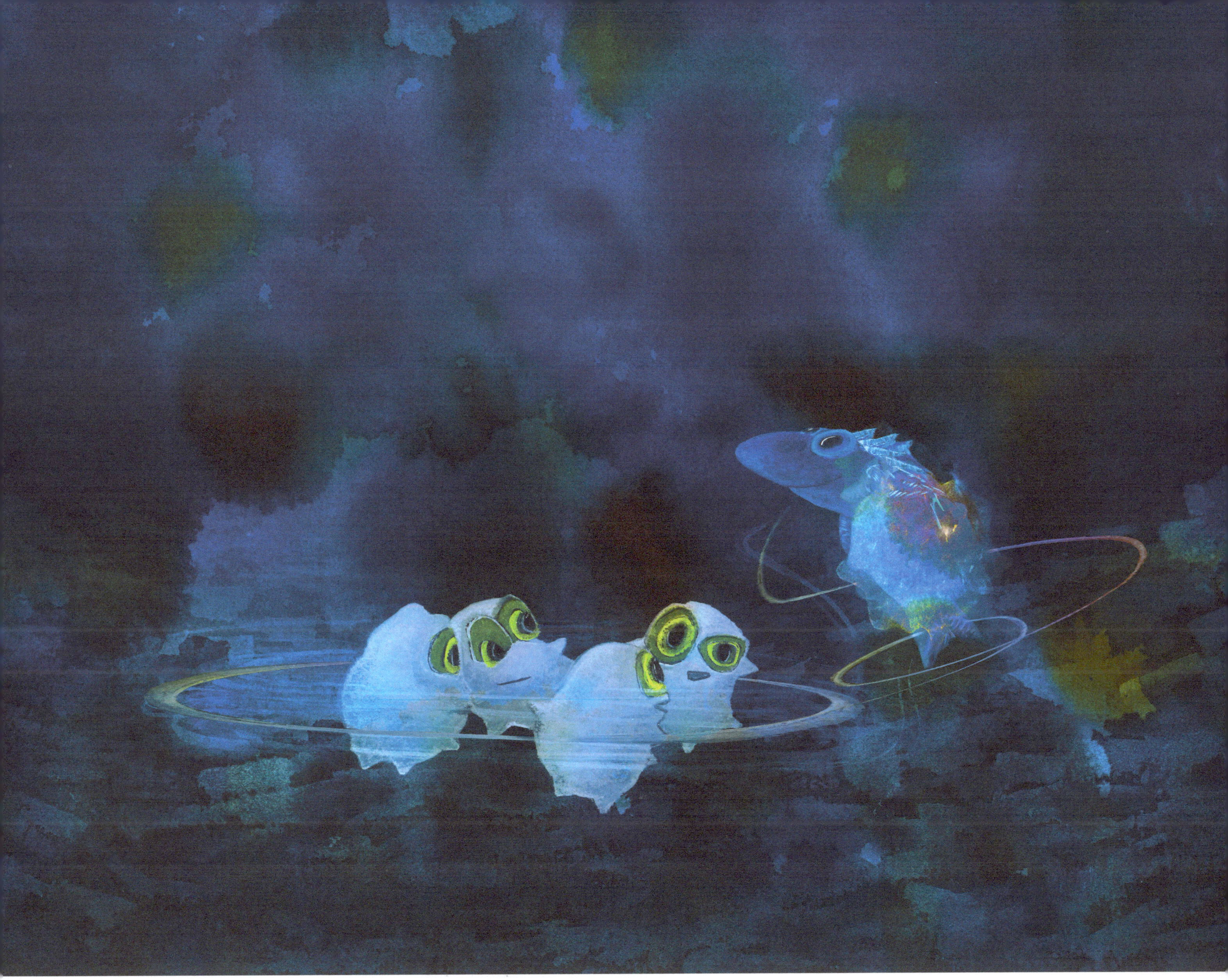

"Grandpa! Where's the surface?" cried Bobi.
Grandpa pointed one tentacle straight up.

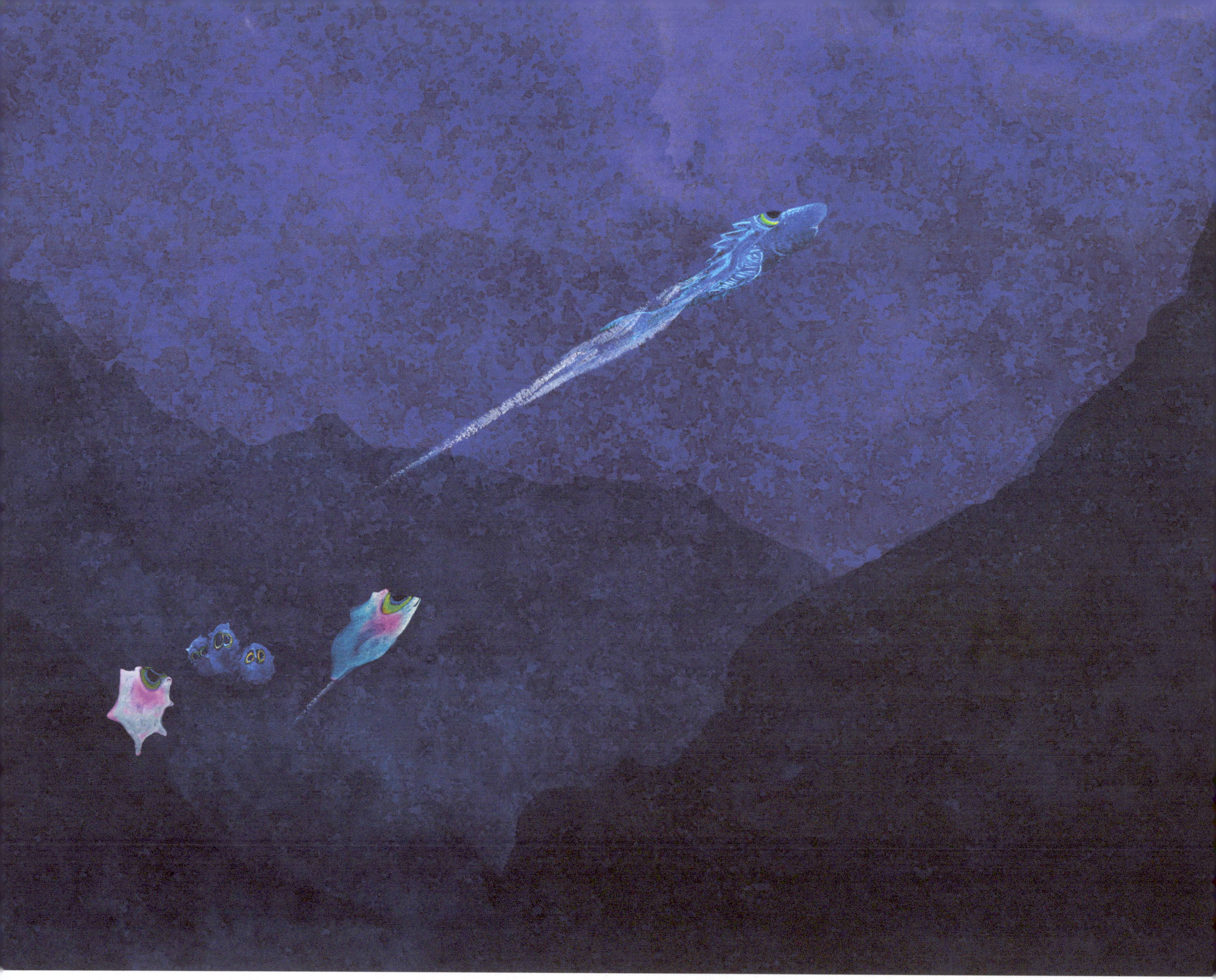

Bobi beat his tail and flapped his fins as fast as he could.

up
    up
        up
            up in the water he rose, higher and higher 'til the dark faded behind him and he burst through the water into the sunlight.

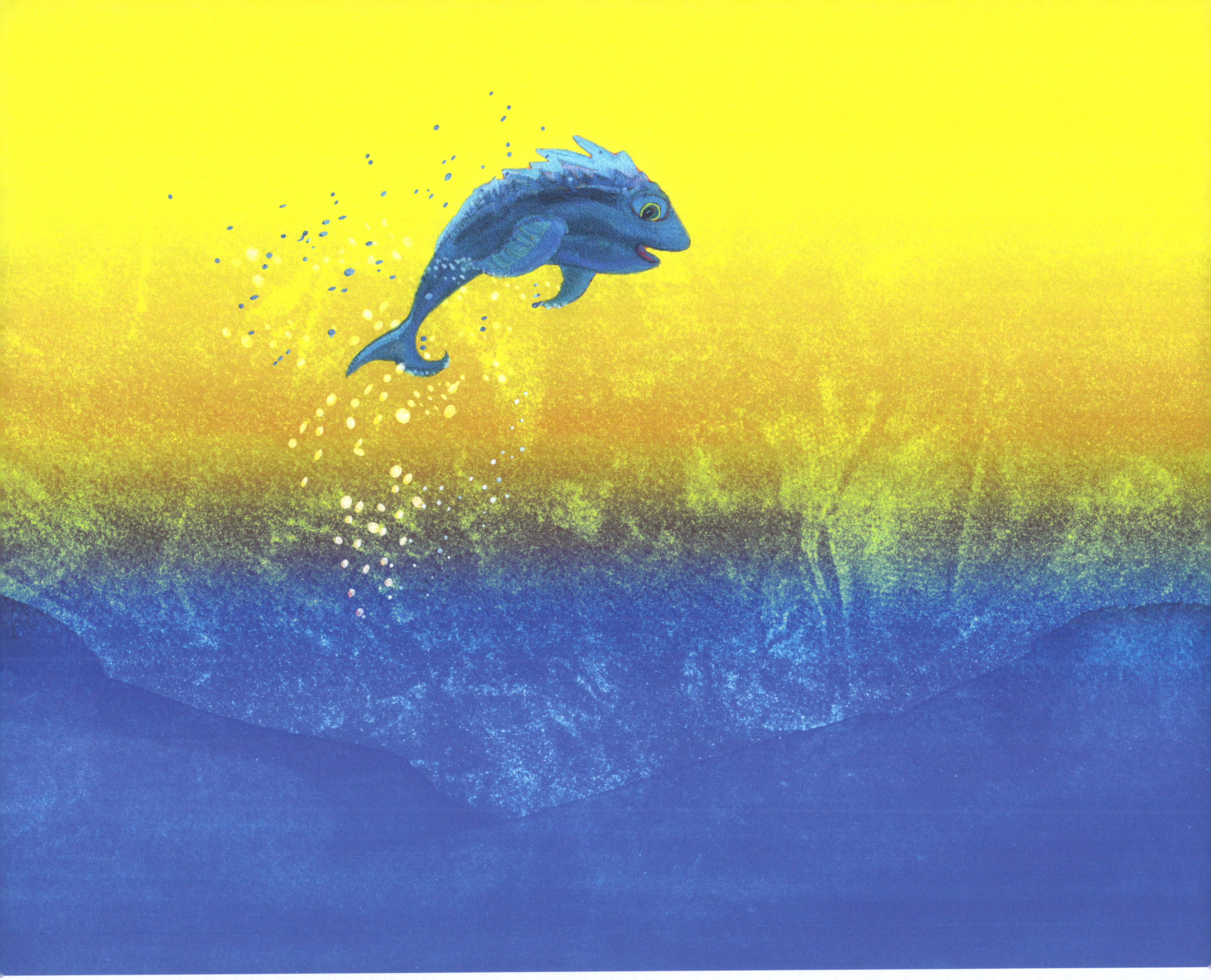

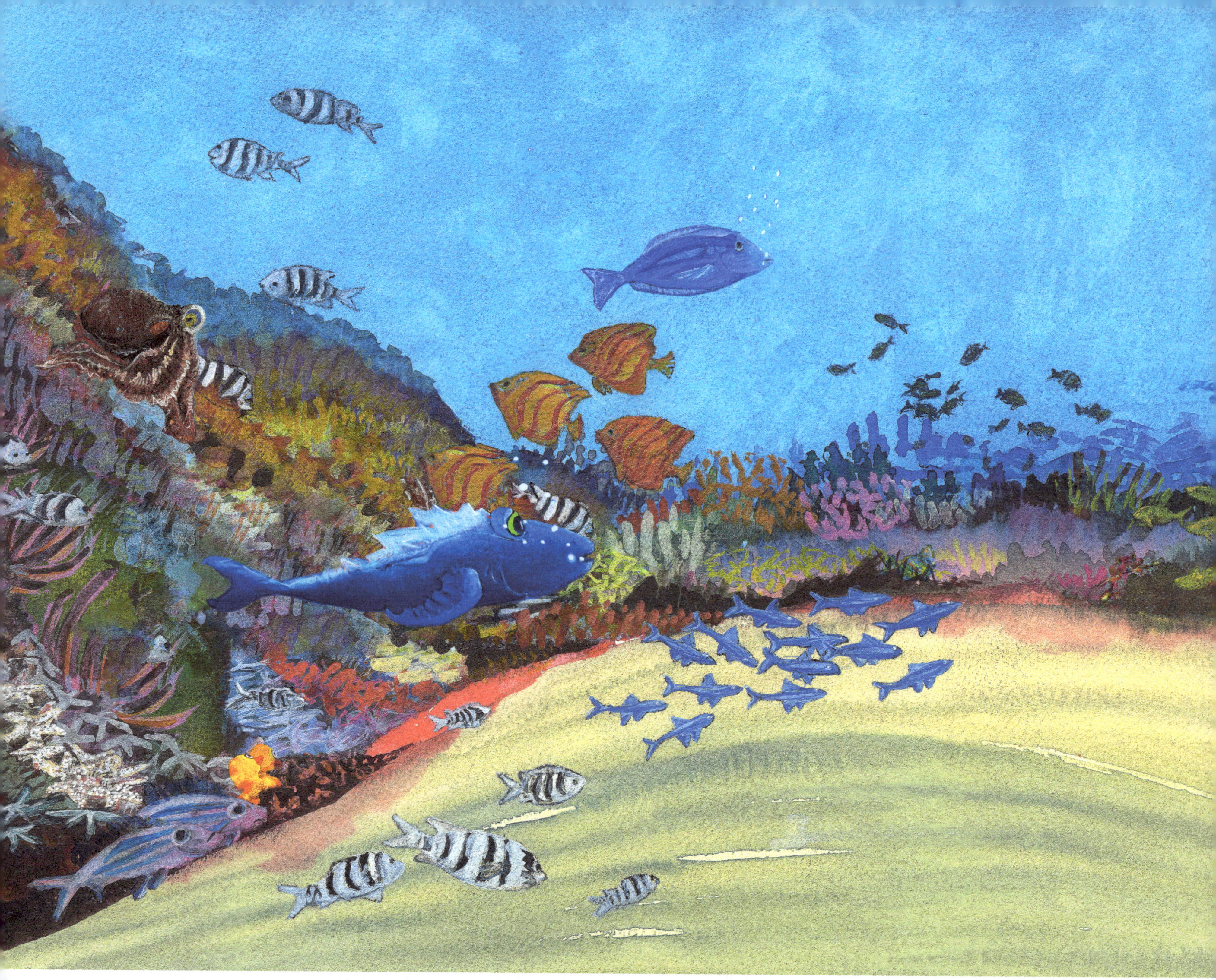

And into an ocean filled with creatures of all shapes and sizes.

THE END

We dedicate this book to Luka and Rafa and all the children that will inheret the earth. May they be creative, full of love and knowledge.

CPSIA information can be obtained
at www.ICGtesting.com
Printed in the USA
BVHW091051240223
659163BV00003B/133